HISTORY OF THE
TOWN OF GREENOCK

HISTORY

OF THE

TOWN OF GREENOCK.

BY DANIEL WEIR.

"Where'er I roam, whatever realms I see,
My heart, untravell'd, fondly turns to thee ;
Still to my youthful scenes with ceaseless pain,
And drags at each remove a lengthening chain."

NEW EDITION.

INTRODUCTORY ESSAY BY CHRIS MORRISON.

PAISLEY:
THE GRIAN PRESS
2004

First published 1829

This edition 2004
Some revisions made December 2004
Published by The Grian Press
7 New Street
Paisley PA1 1XU
Scotland UK

ISBN: 0954799615

Reasonable effort has been made to seek permission to print the poem
"Our River: Greenock.," the publisher of which is unknown.

CONTENTS.

*   *   *   *   *

LIST OF ILLUSTRATIONS.

There are several steel engravings in Weir's history. Excluding the copper-engraved plan, and the view from Mr. Heron's Observatory which was engraved by James Kerr, all are by Joseph Swan. In the original work they are listed as follows:

In this new edition some of the illustrations have been digitally cleaned and reproduced as follows:

ORIGINAL INTRODUCTION BY DANIEL WEIR.

IN presenting this first "History of the Town of Greenock" to the notice of the public, the Author is perfectly aware that many motives may be assigned for so doing. But what led to this attempt, was the fact that many places, less entitled to notice than this flourishing sea-port town, had their rise and progress set before the public, while here we were comparatively unknown. Whether this brief sketch will find its way to any thing like a favourable reception from the public, remains to be seen; and the Author is perfectly aware that there are many individuals in the community more qualified to do justice to the task than he who has drawn up its pages. But what is "writ is writ." To those gentlemen who favoured him with communications to the queries sent abroad, it is but too little to return his most sincere thanks. To William Macfie, Esq., of Langhouse; as also to John Speirs, Esq., M. D.; James Leitch, Esq.; John Mennons, Esq.; Robert Carswell, Esq.; Mr. William Heron, and Mr. Colin Buchanan; it is but justice to state, that their information on various subjects was of the greatest use, and consequently made available in this compilation. Various sources of information have been gone carefully over; and this work has been in no small degree indebted to "Crawford's Renfrewshire;" as Woodrow's Church History;" "Chalmers' Caledonia;" "History of Scotland;" and "Sir John Sinclair's Statistical Account." If any thing is to be regretted, it is the seeming want of arrangement which may appear in the work; and this has arisen, in a great measure, from information coming in when the book itself was in progress through the press. In regard to errors, it is hardly to be expected that a first attempt at history can be entirely free; but whoever maybe called upon to write a second edition, either soon or at a more distant period, can avail himself of such information as the present volume contains, and on this a fabric may be reared more worthy of public support. To the numerous friends who came forward to patronize this effort, more than mere gratitude is due; and they may rest assured, that the feeling which the Author entertains of their kindness is not likely to be soon effaced. It is not to be expected that this rallying round an individual should disarm fair and honourable criticism. The book is put forth with the consciousness of its containing many faults; and if any other person had come forward willing to engage in the task, every information and aid would have been given, and a more perfect record might have been produced of the history of a town, which has risen in importance and greatness scarcely equalled by any place in the neighbourhood.

D. W.

DANIEL WEIR & GREENOCK,
by Chris Morrison.

DANIEL WEIR'S history of the town of Greenock was published in 1829; it was the first published history of the town. Daniel Weir of Greenock was the main imprint; the secondary ones being Robertson & Atkinson of Glasgow; John Boyd of Edinburgh and Whittaker & Co. of London. Weir was a bookseller and chart-seller in Greenock and there are references to him in Pigot's and Fowler's directories of the 1820's as operating at different numbers of Cathcart Street. He is also listed as a bookbinder. According to Archibald Brown in his *Early Annals of Greenock,* 1905, Daniel Weir was of the Weirs or M'Nuirs of Cowal. George Black in his monumental, *The Surnames of Scotland,* first printed in 1946, lists MacNuir as a form of MacNair suggesting three origins: *Mac-Iain-uidhir*—'son of dun John;' *M'an-oighre*—'son of the heir' and *Mac-an-fhuibhir*—'son of the smith' or *Mac-an-fhuidhir*—'son of the stranger.' The last two Gaelic names are pronounced Mac-an-ewar. He writes that the Argyll or Cowal sept are associated with the Clan MacNaughton. Archibald Brown comments on the clutch of Greenock historians, himself included, as all hailing from Argyllshire. According to the biographical blurb on contributors in *The Harp of Renfrews-hire*, an anthology of poetry, published in Paisley in 1873, Daniel Weir was the son of a merchant in Greenock. Apprenticed to a bookseller in 1809 he went into business on his own in 1815. He appears to have edited several volumes of poetry for a Glasgow publisher where some of his own poems were published. It is stated he died in 1831 aged thirty-five. Included in the anthology are two poems by Daniel Weir. One is titled *The Midnight Wind* and the other, *The Dying Hour*, is printed underneath and could perhaps be interpreted as a premonition of his death.

THE DYING HOUR

Why does the day, whose date is brief,
Smile sadly o'er the western sea?
Why does the brown autumnal leaf
Hang restless on its parent tree?
Why does the rose, with drooping head,
Send richer fragrance from the bow'r?
Their golden time of life had fled—
It was their dying hour!

Why does the swan's melodious song
Come thrilling on the gentle gale?
Why does the lamb, which stray'd along,
Lie down to tell its mournful tale
Why does the deer, when wounded, fly
To the lone vale, where night-clouds low'r
Their time was past—they lived to die—
It was their dying hour!

Why does the dolphin change its hues,
Like that aerial child of light?
Why does the cloud of night refuse
To meet the morn with beams so bright
Why does the man we saw to-day,
To-morrow fade like some sweet flow'r?
All earth can give must pass away
It was their dying hour !

It's not the cheeriest of poems but bear in mind the possible state of the poet's mind. He died young as many did in those times. Judging by the lack of organization in his history it does seem that Weir was in a hurry to see publication of his work. This was not his first publication; in 1825, while at 3 Cathcart Street, he published a *New Universal or Perpetual Tide Table on an Improved Principle and Complete Course and Distance Book for the Whole Coasts of Europe... Containing in an Appendix the Courses and Distances up the River to Greenock.*

The 1829 first edition of the history is a scarce book today. The book was reprinted in 1917 by The Greenock Herald Office. This edition although calling itself a facsimile edition lacked reproductions of the original illustrations; the notes had also been omitted although the errata had been incorporated. The Grian Press 2004 edition has reproduced the original illustrations in our own style. The engravings have been digitally cleaned. A comprehensive index has also been added.

The printing of books in Greenock appears to have began in 1778, the earliest recorded printing being by William M'Alpine, also a bookseller, having the sugary-sweet title, "Poems full of gospel-marrow and sweet invitations to heaven's happiness" by William Tenent. This rare book, not one that would attract a queue of avid readers, was acquired by the National Library of Scotland in the year 1997-98 being previously unrecorded in their collections. The title is taken from the NLS online catalogue. Archibald Brown, eager, as always, to show the input of the Highlander to Greenock's history, refers to this book as "Poems full of Gospel Marrow and Sweet Invitations to Heaven's Blessing, composed by W. Tenent, Wheelright in Glasgow, and copied by John Finlayson, Schoolmaster at Kilern." Since I have not seen a copy I cannot say which title is correct, or indeed, if they are both correct. Errors can be perpetuated by writers referring to books referred to in other books and it is a cardinal rule of some bibliographers to physically handle the book they are listing and describing. In Greenock's printing history this rarity was followed by "Genuine Narratives and Concise Memoirs of some of the most interesting exploits and singular adventures of J.

M'Alpine, a native Highlander, from the time of his emigration from Scotland to America, 1773," also printed by W. M'Alpine. We are curious to learn if author and publisher were related. This book appears to be an account of a Scottish Highlander during the American War of Independence.

One of the better known early printers and booksellers in Greenock was William Scott. As well as larger works, Scott printed quite a number of chapbooks from around 1810-1830, usually ranging from eight to twenty-four pages in length with a crude or naive woodcut on the title page.[1] The intriguing material was of general interest with the odd one being specifically related to Greenock, like "..the last moments and execution of Moses M'Donald who was executed in Greenock for housebreaking and theft in 1812." This would have been the popular literature that Daniel Weir grew up amongst. It seems rather odd that Daniel Weir writes as Scott printing the first book in Greenock— *Hutcheson's Dissertation.* One would think that as a bookseller he would have been aware of M'Alpine's printed books. He does acknowledge M'Alpine, spelled Macalpine, as being the first printer in Greenock, a letterpress printer commencing in 1765, who printed posters and handbills and items of ephemera. He also acknowledges him as first bookseller. There must have been a very small number of the first books he printed. Perhaps they had entirely disappeared out of circulation by Daniel Weir's time, some 50 years or so later.

As a bookseller Daniel Weir would have been aware of the interest shown in extant printed histories of towns. He tells us that some of his facts came from old inhabitants of the town and was shrewd enough to understand the importance of these local histor-

---

1. A checklist of Chapbooks printed by Willam Scott of Greenock has
    been compiled by E.B. Lyle in *The Bibliotheck* Volume 10, No. 2
    1980.

ical gleanings being documented for posterity. He was conscious of the fact that his work would be the very first history of Greenock printed and comments on the fact that histories had been written of places of lesser importance than that of the "flourishing sea-port town" as he terms Greenock. The subscribers list printed at the end of this edition accounts for a total of well over 600 copies subscribed by just under 450 individuals. Of these approximately 1/12th ordered multiple copies, many of whom were booksellers, or printers as publishers were then known. Some well known names are apparent, like Oliver and Boyd who developed into a major Edinburgh-based publisher, or the Lumsdens, publishers of the popular steamboat companion, an item that Daniel Weir in role of bookseller would have regularly handled. The copy of Weir's history that was used to prepare this edition was specially bound in a tooled, full leather binding with an embossed title, as shown on the illustration underneath: This

binding would have been crafted for the owner of a Steam-Boat by name of *Conqueror* which presumably sailed to and from Greenock. The book would would have been found in the ship's library for crew and passengers to read. The subscribers list reveals local trade names like William Scott, bookseller, among others. Some eminent private individuals were subscribers. Sir Walter Scott was one, a father figure of the Scottish historical novel. Always receptive to potential sources of history and legend, Scott, who was to die later in 1832, would have been busy with his *History of Scotland* (1829-30) and still popular *Tales of a Grandfather* (1828-30). In 1814, just two years after the appearance of The Comet on the Clyde, Sir Walter Scott sailed from Greenock to Glasgow on a steamboat, an experience he clearly relished. Francis Jeffrey the critic and editor, founder member of The Edinburgh Review, a man who had a distaste for the Scottish accent, the one who penned the inscription above the entrance to the Watt Institution in Union Street. Another subscriber was Archibald Robertson, Liverpool, the Greenockian wood-carver who specialised in ship figureheads, best known in Renfrewshire as the artist who carved the likeness of Kilbarchan's famous piper, Habbie Simpson. The total number of subscribers gives us some idea of the size of the print run which was probably close to a thousand copies. The market was predominantly a national one, wider than that of Scott's chapbooks and although Weir's book would not have the immediate, popular appeal of the chapbook, it would stand the test of time in enduring interest. And so it has.

Local history, like family history, has never been so alive as it is today. Reminiscence groups abound capturing memories of the older members of the community. Courses are run on the subject at universities. In fact the University of Paisley started one a few years ago.

The 60's and 70's saw the needless destruction of many properties of local historic interest to make way for some planned building, devoid of character and history, that soon became an eyesore. Decisions were later regretted. However, times change and we would like to think we are now in an age of conservation where old, interesting historic properties are, hopefully, saved and restored. Conversions to make comfortable, habitable dwelling places are made from old churches and mills, byres & barns, warehouses, hospitals & schools, coach-houses & stables, and other old buildings. People who subsequently live in these conversions may ask questions about the local and family history. It might be about the place-name of the locality, the street or the property, the previous owners or the architects—who they were and how they lived and what interested them, and so we come back, full circle, to the importance of Weir's history as an attempt to document the local history of Greenock up to 1829. Family historians refer to local histories during their research. They can yield all kinds of information: the subscribers list for instance is what genealogists would see as a primary source, in the same way they would an early trade directory. You can see clutches of names associated with Greenock, like the McCunns, a name made famous by the work of the Greenockian composer, Hamish MacCunn (1868-1916), son of a ship-owner in Greenock who married the daughter of the Scottish artist, John Pettie. The index added in this new edition is designed for the benefit of local and family historians; almost every name in the book has been added and it reads like a directory as well as an index.

Scotland in the early 19th century was a rather poor place with high unemployment. The Napoleonic wars had drained the purse of the country. The numbers of Irish immigrants arriving, Catholic and Protestant, escaping an impoverished Ireland, were not welcome because of the scarcity of jobs. The British government was trying to claw back revenue to re-build its reserves. Officials set about to achieve this by such means as the Corn Law of 1815, a law that proved incendiary to a nation with towns that had been fomenting radicalism for some years. *The Society of Friends of the People* founded in 1792 saw radical members like Thomas Muir of Huntershill being tried for sedition. The Peterloo massacre in Manchester, 1819, caused the Paisley Radicals to drill more intensely so the historian, Parkhill, wrote in his history of Paisley. The memories of the fate of the martyrs: Baird, Hardie and Wilson, all executed in 1820 for their part in struggling for egalitarian ideals are indelibly etched in the psyche of the Scottish people. Greenock experienced a tragic affair in 1820 when Radical leaders taken prisoner were transferred to Greenock jail from Paisley, the jail there being apparently overcrowded. Weir writes that there were only 3 radicals but in the detailed although somewhat confusingly presented work by Peter Berresford Ellis and Seumas Mac A'Ghobhainn—*The Scottish Insurrection of 1820*—it is stated that 5 prisoners were being transferred. They were escorted to jail by the militia through a hostile crowd who then marched back through the town. Provoked by jeers and taunts and missiles thrown at them the militia starting firing into the crowd. A number of people were shot dead, some dying of their wounds, while others were seriously wounded. Later the crowd enraged by the day's events (led by a piper whose martial music would put fire into their veins) eventually freed the leaders of the Radicals, only one of which was apparently ever recaptured. The fact is that none of the troops who fired on the crowd were ever brought to justice over the affair, no compensation was paid to the victims' families, and to this day no memorial exists to the memory in those poor people who died as working class martyrs.

These seeds of discontent, fuelled by thinkers like Thomas Paine and William Cobbett (and let us not forget the Spirit of Robert Burns that had been earlier unleashed upon the Scottish people) and the events of the French and American revolutions, led to constant clamour for political reform; the right to vote for all was a burning issue, paving the way for the Reform Act of 1832. The Industrial Revolution was moving into a higher gear; factories in central locations in towns were manufacturing, replacing the work of the individual carried out in cottages in the small villages, another source of unrest. James Watt, perhaps Greenock's greatest son, was a father figure of this new day of the machine.

The Greenock of 1829 was that of a very busy sea-port although Glasgow's dependence on the towns on the Firth was declining with the setting up of the River Improvement Trust in 1809 for the purpose of deepening the Clyde.

Just imagine taking a stroll along one of the harbours, perhaps the town's first constructed West Harbour. Limbless veterans from the Napoelonic wars who may have seen action at the battle of Trafalgar would be hobbling around the stone quays. Daniel Weir writes that it was in the arms of a Greenockian seaman that the intrepid Admiral Horatio Nelson was cradled while being conveyed to the cockpit after receiving his death-wound, a shot on the left shoulder, on the quarterdeck of *The Victory*. Salty dogs—old, wizened mariners, full of tales, whose sea-faring days were over, would be sitting, looking out to the Tail of the Bank, wistfully watching the busy traffic of barques, brigs, cutters, square-riggers, sloops, schooners and steamboats that were plying their trade to and from distant lands, or closer home to another bustling port of the day like Liverpool. A poem that attempts to capture that spirit, albeit of a somewhat later vintage than the time we are at, was written by a John Gillespie. He privately published a volume of poems in Greenock in 1937. One is called "Our River: Greenock" and paints a quaint picture of the myriad forms of vessels strutting their stuff on the Clyde at Greenock.

Our River: Greenock

A game old dredger's sump-clank,
A puffer 'cross Gareloch's mouth,
Tide-set prowed by the Tail-o'-the-Bank,

A great white ship from the south;
A long, weird hoot thro' the haze of morn,
An early fisher spume breaking clever,
And that's how day is born,
On the river.

Some great, gaunt trader from Spain
With stern swerve shaped as a jug,
A coaster fresh from the main,
The finch-wing lines of a tug;
Long drawn bow lights of the bay,
A smack with her cloth a-quiver,
And day slips away,
On the river.

The Tail-o'-the-Bank is the beginning of the sand bank, formed just off Greenock and acquired formally as Greenock's in 1817. The cover illustrations, slightly smaller reproductions of the engraved originals, show a number of types of ships. You can see the different riggings which is how sailing ships are defined. Allmost all would have wonderfully carved, garishly painted figureheads, a maritime tradition of great antiquity that captivated the wood carver, Archibald Robertson, whom Weir mentions carved a likeness of shipbuilder, John Scott, for the ship of that name. This ancient art, steeped in mythology and folklore, had all but ceased by the early twentieth century. Watching the ships go by from The Esplanade, with its splendid panorama, is still a timeless, leisurely pursuit. But, alas, the vessels are fewer and not near as outwardly interesting.

But back to our quay: Urchins in rags would be begging farthings from the able, bearded seamen as they went briskly about their business, perhaps eying up an opportunity to jump aboard a ship as a stowaway. Young stowaways were a constant problem for the authorities. What is this romance, this yearning, that has made so many young men run away to sea to seek their fortune among the salty waves? Some ended up pirates and buccaneers. What went wrong in the life of the infamous Captain William Kidd, himself a native of Greenock? Also conscious of these wayward youngsters would be the brightly buttoned, uniformed, Customs and Excise men who would be vigilantly inspecting newly arrived vessels for contraband. The smuggling of illicit substances was as popular then as it is now. The interesting collections housed within the museum of the Custom House Quay building today are testament to this statement. But far worse than the smugglers were the kidnappers. You might glimpse sight of a desperately, anxious young woman searching for her lover who had been press-ganged into naval service. Ralph Vaughan Williams in Sussex, 1904, collected the poignant air, now a well-known English folk-song, "All Things are Quite Silent" that describes the horror of being press-ganged.

> All things are quite silent, each mortal at rest,
> When me and my love got snug in one nest,
> When a bold set of ruffians broke into our cave,
> And they forced my dear jewel to plough the salt wave.
>
> I begged hard for my darling as I would for my life.
> But they'd not listen to me although a fond wife,
> Saying: "The king must have sailors, to the seas he must go,"
> And they've left me lamenting in sorrow and woe.
>
> Through green fields and meadows we oftimes have walked,
> And the fond recollections together have talked,
> Where the lark and the blackbird so sweetly did sing,
> And the lovely thrushes' voices made the valleys to ring.
>
> Now although I'm forsaken, I won't be cast down.
> Who knows but my true love some day may return

And will make me amends for my trouble and strife,
And me and my true love might live happy for life.

Actually, there is a song extant that tells the story of being press-ganged in Greenock. It was written by one Dòmhnall MacMhuirich, or Donald Currie, from Ballymichael on the Isle of Arran. Traditionally the clan MacMhuirich was an illustrious bardic dynasty spanning several centuries. Based in Kintyre, they were hereditary bards to the Lords of the Isles until the forfeiture of the Lordship in 1493. They then became bards to Clanranald and moved to Stilligarry, South Uist. Donald Currie of Arran was nabbed during the times of the Napoleonic wars by a press-gang. The song is taken from *The Book of Arran* volume two, published in Glasgow for the Arran Society in 1914.

Là is Mi a' Sràideas ann an Grianaig
One Day While Sauntering through Greenock

Là 's mi 'sràideas ann an Grianaig
'S gun mo smaointean air na biastan
'Sann a thàinig iad mar mhialchoin
Is spiol iad mi gun tròcair

One day while sauntering through Greenock
With no thoughts of the 'beasts'
How they came like hunting dogs
And ensnared me mercilessly

Ha u rillean agus ho!
Ha u rillean agus ho!
I rillean agus hog i o
Mo chridhe trom 's mi brònach

Ha u rillean agus ho!

Ha u rillean agus ho!
I rillean agus hog i o!
My heart is heavy and I am sad

Thàinig fear dhiubh air gach taobh dhiom
'S iad le'n lannan biorach geur leò
Is thàin' an treas fear as mo dhèidh
'S feitheamh ri mo leònadh

One of them came on each side of me
Carrying their sharp pointy blades
And the third one came after me
Intending to wound me

'S on a chunnaic Bennie 'chuideachd
Gam shlaodadh leò air mhuineal
'Sann a ghlaodh e: "S math na curaidhean,
Cuireamaid air bòrd e"

Since Bennie saw the company
Dragging me by the throat
He shouted: "What good soldiers,
Let's put him on board"

Chuir iad mi don gheòla chaoil
'S dh'iomair iad mi gus an taobh
Is nach robh fear dhiubh air mo thaobh
'S b'èiginn dhomh dol leòcha

They sent me to the narrow boat
And rowed me over to their side
Not a man of them was my ally
And I had to go along with them

Nuair a ràinig sinn a gualann
'Sann a ghlaodh iad rium dol suas innt'

Air m' fhìrinn-se gum b'e bu chruaidhe
Na bhith buain na mòine

When we reached her (the ship's) bow
They yelled to me to go up into her
On my word it was harder
Than cutting the peats

Nuair a ràinig sinn air bòrd
Cha robh truas ac' do m' dheòir
Ach 'sann a mhionnaich iad mo sheòrs'
Gun robh Deòrsa gann dhiubh

When we came on board
They had no pity for my tears
They cursed my sort
George's ranks were short-supplied

Thug iad sìos mi don phress room
'S bha gach aon dhiubh feòrachd ceist dhiom
An do ghabh mi bunndaist no 'n do list mi
No 'n e 'm press thug leò mi

They took me down to the press-room
Each one was asking me questions
Did I get a fee or did I enlist
Or did the press gang take me with them

Ach dh'innis mise dhaibh an fhìrinn
Air dol leò nach robh mo smaointean
'S ged a fhuair iad mi 'nan ìnean
Nach robh mìr de dheòin orm

But I told the truth to them
That my thoughts were not of going with them
Although they had me in their claws

I was not one bit willing

'S ged a fhuair mi deoch is biadh ann
'S nach robh tùrn agam ri dhèanadh
B'annsa leam bhith gu mo shliasaid
Ann an sliabh na mòine

And although I got food and drink there
And although I had no chores to do
I would prefer to be up to my thighs
In the peat moor

Thoir mo shoraidh bhuam gu Raghnall
Agus innis mar a tha mi
'S nan do ghabh mi 'chomhairle tràth
Nach robh mi 'n-dràst cho brònach

Take my greetings to Ronald
And relate how I am
And that had I taken his advice before
That I would not be so sorry now

The press-gangs, or Impress Service as Weir refers to them, operated nation-wide but had all but faded away by the mid 1830's. Notice that there is a reference to "Bennie" in the above song of bitterness and regret. This Lieutenant Benny was a notorious leader of a press gang in Greenock. Archibald Brown writes he also kept a public-house in the Vennel full of spies loyal to him who helped ensnare and kidnap seafaring men who were then dragged aboard warships sitting at the Tail-o'-the-Bank. These thugs were detested by the people of Greenock and Daniel Weir does describe some riots that took place as a result of their nefarious practices.

The harbours of Greenock in Daniel Weir's day would have been full of characters that would have fuelled the imaginations of writers like Robert Louis Stevenson or Joseph Conrad. Stevenson sailed from the Broomielaw, Glasgow to Greenock en route to America in 1879.

The bard in the poem above refers to Greenock in Gaelic as 'Grianaig.' Literally this means 'sun-at', 'aig' (at) being a simple preposition showing possession of 'grian' (sun). However, it is thought that the 'aig' is from the Norse 'vik,' for bay, making the name an understandable 'sunny-bay.' Another possible interpretation is 'sunny-hill' from the Gaelic, 'cnoc,' for hill. There was a private press called Grian-aig Press which was established by Thomas Rae in 1967 in Greenock, replacing another private press he had run called the Signet Press. The Grian-aig press closed in 1973 after producing five books. In 1982 Thomas Rae created The Black Pennel Press producing more examples of fine design, typography and printing.

Many Gaelic speaking families, victims of the clearances or lured by the prospect of a brighter future, would have departed from Greenock in the 18th and 19th centuries for a new life in distant lands. Pictou, Nova Scotia was a frequent destination of the emigrant ships like that of the Hector. The voyages were tough and many died of hunger and disease along the way. Some of the eye-witness descriptions of the pitiful conditions of the poor people are heart-rending. The harbours of Greenock have seen so many poignant farewells of loved ones, sometimes to be later joyfully re-united or perhaps never seen again. Many songs of parting have been silently sung on these harbours from women seeing their menfolk off to war to divided families seeing part of them leave for foreign soil. This theme has inspired countless poets throughout time. Perhaps one of the greatest songs of parting is *Ae Fond Kiss* by Robert Burns. A plaintive and evocative air that describes the separation and longing for home of an emigrant to Canada is (first 3 verses only):

Oh Mo Dhuthaich
(O My Country)

Ó mo dhùthaich, 'stu th'air m'aire
Uibhist chùmhraidh ùr nan gallan
Far a faighte na daoin' uaisle
Far 'm bu dual do Mhac 'ic Ailein

Oh my country, you are on my mind
Fresh, fragrant Uist of the saplings
Where the noble men are found
Who gave their hereditary allegiance to Mac ic Ailein

Tìr a' mhurain, tìr an eorna
Tìr 's am pailt a h-uile seòrsa
Far am bi na gillean òga
Gabhail òran 's 'g òl an lionna

Land of seabed, land of barley
Land of abundance of every kind
Where the young lads will be
Singing songs and drinking beer

Thig iad ugainn, carach, seòlta
Gus ar mealladh far ar n-eòlais
Molaidh iad dhuinn Manitòba
Dùthaich fhuar gun ghual, gun mhòine

They come to us, cunning and wily
In order to entice us from our homes
They will praise Manitoba to us
A cold country with no coal and no peat

We can only wonder how many songs like this were sung by
emigrants who parted Scotland from Greenock never to return.

Daniel Weir occasionally writes with a humour betraying a love of his town and its character-fashioned style: he likens two tradesmen, a smith and the tailor, to Tam O'Shanter and Souter Johnny, the couthie drinking cronies. When drunk they argue over the name of a new street where both have premises: the tailor wants the street named Needle Street while the smith favours, Hammer Street. We detect some mirth too on the subject of the windows of an early inn providing "a faithful, though brittle record, of the love effusions of its wayfaring inhabitants," evidence that Greenockians liked to laugh at life as much then as they do now.

The original text has been adhered to as closely as possible. A few obvious misprints have been corrected. Some hyphenated street names have been split for the sake of consistency. Slang or variant spellings have been left for their quaint appeal. A small number of footnotes have been added by us, recognisable by the letters, GP. We regret the presence of any typos that have crept in and slipped through our net while preparing this new edition.

In his introduction Daniel Weir is at pains to apologise for the lack of organization of his work, citing the manner in which the information was received as being the reason. It is hoped that this new edition, which has been ordered into clearly, demarcated chapters, will help those readers who previously had been intimidated by the seemingly, never-ending, rambling style. It is equally hoped that new readers will find Daniel Weir's history of the town of Greenock an interesting account of a fascinating town.

Chris Morrison
THE GRIAN PRESS
Paisley December 2004

HISTORY

OF THE

TOWN OF GREENOCK.

Embosom'd in a lovely bay,
We see thy crowded mansions rise;
While commerce, with her proud display,
Arrests at once our wondering eyes.

These are the fleets which plow the main,
And visit isles beyond the sea;
Yet homeward turn their prow again,
To waft their treasures back to thee.

Twas this which made thee what thou art,
A child of wealth tho' young in years;
And bade thee into being start,
From that which scarcely now appears.

The huts are gone—the spire is seen,
The glebe resounds with infant glee;
And where the proud oak wav'd with green,
No vestige of its pride we see.

All, all around bespeaks thee great,
And may thy wealth with years extend;
An arm to shield our parent state,
While King and country call thee friend!

Chapter 1.
THE LANDOWNERS.

IN writing a history of Greenock, it cannot be expected that there
will be much to interest the lovers of antiquarian lore: its origin is

but of recent date; and its progressive improvement, from a small fishing village to its present state, has been but little more than the work of a century. Few places in the empire have made more rapid advances towards commercial importance, and no sea-port in Scotland produces greater revenues from the duties levied by the Excise and Customs. Its trade extends to every part in the world, and, during the long and arduous wars, our seamen were alike famed for their noble daring in fighting the battles of our country, as they were for their skill and enterprise in visiting foreign climates, which to many proved only but a grave.

The name *Greenock* is derived from the British *Graenag*, signifying a gravelly or sandy place, or from the Gaelic *Grain-ach*, signifying a *sunny place*. Either of these derivations is sufficiently applicable, as it has a gravelly or sandy soil, and is exposed to the rising sun which it receives on the bosom of its beautiful bay. Notwithstanding of this, a popular opinion has gone abroad that the origin of the name arose from a fine spreading oak, which stood at the foot of William Street, and to which the fishing boats used to be fastened, but this is a mere quibble. "What sort of an oak is Gourock? and what Garvock?—these are both in the neighbourhood."

Greenock is confined on the north by the sea, and on the south-west by a range of hills, which take their rise about Finlayston, stretching along to the height of eight hundred feet,[1] and terminate near Gourock. In consequence of this peculiarity, the town originally stretched in a line along the shore, and including Crawfordsdyke, may be considered at present to extend in length to about two and a half miles, while its breadth is inconsiderable.

For so high a latitude the weather is generally mild, the most prevalent winds being from the southward and westward; and

---

1.   Corlic is considered the highest elevation, and presents a most
      delightful view.

though abundantly changeable, the extremes of heat and cold are not very great. The thermometer rarely rises above 80.0 of Fahrenheit.—In the hot summer of 1826, it sometimes stood at 82.0 or 83.0; and once as high as 85.0. During frost in winter this instrument seldom falls under 20 degrees, and once only during the last ten years has it been down to 15.0. When southerly winds prevails in winter, the weather is commonly moist and mild. In the month of January last, the thermometer on one occasion stood at 55.0, and at the same season of the year it is frequently above 50.0, even at midnight.

Greenock, notwithstanding the eminence to which it has attained, is entirely of modern creation, and it is only about 160 years since its whole buildings consisted of a row of houses near the Rue-end, and at intervals, till they reached near the West Quay head. The first feu which was granted, was in 1636, at the foot of the "Broomy brae," or what is now called the Tan-work closs. But though the parish of Greenock is of modern origin, the barony is of very ancient date. Crawfurd says:—

"A mile west off Port-Glasgow, upon the shore, stands the ruinous castle of Easter-Greenock,[1] a possession till of late, and for 300 years past, of the Crawfurds of Kilbirny; which came to that family by right of marriage of . . . Galbraith, daughter, and one of the coheirs, of Malcolm Galbraith of Greenock, in the reign King Robert III. The common ancestor of the Crawfurds, as our renown'd Historian and Antiquary Mr. Thomas Crawfurd, Professor of Philosophy and Mathematicks in the University of Edinburgh, and author of the Notes on Buchanan's History (who also wrote an Historical account of some of the ancient families of his name), says, was one Mackornock; who, as the story goes, signalized himself at an engagement by the water of Cree in

---

1. About 60 years ago the late tenant of Hill-end, where stood the ancient Castle of Greenock, in excavating the ground, fell in with a sunk cellar, where was found a number of casks containing liquid, the nature of which could not be ascertained.

Galloway, by discovering of a Foord, which gave a signal advantage to
his party. The story may carry some show of truth; for it is observed,
that most of our surnames at first were taken from places, accidents, and
the most remarkable actions of a man's life; but this I wave, as not being
so well attested.

"But the first using this sirname, I have found, is Galfridus de
Crawfurd, who is witness in a charter by Roger Bishop of St. Andrews,
to the Abbacy of Kelso, declaring that Monastery independent of the
Episcopal See. Which charter has probably been about the year 1189,
when Roger was elected Bishop of St. Andrews, in the reign of King
William; so it is clear that the family of Crawfurd, seated at a place of
that name, in the county of Lanerk, and from their hereditary lands took
designation, when fixed surnames came commonly to be used. But the
principal family of this name failed in the reign of King Alexander II, in
the person of Sir John Crawfurd of that ilk, who departed this life in an.
1248. His estate went to his daughters and co-heirs; Margaret the elder
being married to Hugh de Douglas, ancestor of the Duke of Douglas;
and the second daughter married David de Lindsay, ancestor to the Earl
of Crawfurd.

"The principal family of the Crawfurds thus failing, a part of the old
estate remained with the male issue of the ancient proprietors, as the
learned Sir James Dalrymple observes. For, in a donation by David de
Lindsay to the Monastery of Newbottle, out of the lands of Crawfurd, he
bounds his gift 'inter terram meam terram Johannis, filii Reginaldi de
Crawford, usque ad terram Ecclesiae de Crawfurd.' That the lands of
John, the son of Reginald de Crawfurd, are excepted out of the foresaid
donation, the same celebrated author thinks, gave rise to the distinction
of the lands of Crawfurd Lindsay, from Crawfurd John.

"And that a family of the sirname of Crawfurd had possession in
Clydesdale, near Crawfurd, and a distinct family from the Crawfurds of
Loudoun, who was the first and most considerable branch of the princi-
pal stemm, and seated in the shire of Air, while the family of Crawfurd
of that ilk existed, the following authority will sufficiently document.
For Mr. Thomas Crawfurd, our learned Antiquary and Historian, makes
Loudoun's ancestor grand uncle to Sir John the last Baron of Crawfurd;
and in the reign of King Alexander II. 'Reginaldus de Crawfurd,

Vicecomes de Air,' who is of Loudoun, is frequently mention'd in the Registers of the Abbies of Kelso and Pasly, about the year 1226, and in the same reign obtained the Barony of Loudoun, by marriage of the heiress of James Loudoun of that ilk, of whom the right honourable Hugh Earl of Loudoun is the lineal heir. So that I think probably John, the son of Reginald de Crawfurd, who had lands contiguous to the Barony of Crawfurd, mentioned from the Chartulary of Newbottle, was a son of the first Sir Reginald Crawfurd of Loudoun. Moreover I have seen, in the Register of the Abby of Kelso, in the Advocates Library at Edinburgh, a Writ an. 1271, wherein Andrew, Abbot of Kelso, acknowledges 'Dominum Hugonem Crawfurd, Militem, & Aliciam sponsam ejus, in possessione terrae de Draffan, in Vicecomitatu de Lanerk' which lands they held of that Convent. And, that this Sir Hugh Crawfurd was not of Loudoun, our national histories do sufficiently evidence. They mention Sir Reginald Crawfurd of Loudoun the father, and Sir Reginald the son, among other Scots Patriots, who stood firm to the interest of their country, after King Alexander III.'s death, in opposition to the oppression of King Edward I. of England, and were contemporary with Sir Hugh above mentioned.

"There is also extant, in the Viscount of Garnock's Charterchest, a contract of Excambion between Laurence Crawfurd of Kilbirny, his ancestor, upon the one part, and Sir James Hamilton of Finnart, with consent of Margaret Livingston his spouse, upon the other, dated Jan. 29, 1528; whereby Kilbirny excambed his part of the lands of Crawfurd-John, with Sir James Hamilton's lands of Drumray in the shire of Dumbarton; which continues with his descendents, and gives the title of Lord to the Right Honourable Patrick Viscount of Garnock. Which Laurence Crawfurd of Kilbirny, was son and heir of Robert Crawfurd of Kilbirny, by Marion his wife, a daughter of the family of Semple; and he, of John Crawfurd of Kilbirny; and he, of Malcolm Crawfurd of Kilbirny, who obtained the Barony of Kilbirny and diverse other lands, by marriage of Marjory, daughter and sole heir of John Barclay of Kilbirny, who was a branch of the Barclays of Ardrossan, a family of great antiquity in the shire of Air. Richard de Barclay their ancestor, is mentioned a witness in the foundation Charter of the Abby of Kilwinning, founded by Hugh Morvel, Constable of Scotland, in King Malcolm IV.'s time.

"But to return to the family of Kilbirny: Of Laurence abovementioned, I have found nothing more to record, but that in the year 1547, he settled upon his chapel of Drumray, a liberal fund, for the better support of certain Priests to celebrate divine service 'for the soul of his late Sovereign Lord, King James V. and for the good estate of himself, and of Helen Campbel his wife, daughter of Sir Hugh Campbel of Loudoun; and for all the faithful deceased.' He departed this life in the month of June 1547, leaving issue, by the said Helen his wife, Hugh his son and heir; John of Easter Greenock; and Captain Thomas, ancestor of the Crawfurds of Jordanhill and Cartsburn. He had, moreover, a daughter, Catharine, married to David Fairly of that ilk, and had issue.

"To Laurence Crawford of Kilbirny succeeded Hugh his son and heir; who, adhering to the interest of Queen Mary, at the field of Langside, join'd Her Majesty's troops with a considerable number of his vassals; for which he took a Remission from the Regent Lenox, in the year 1571. He was twice married; first, with Margaret, daughter of Sir John Colquhoun of Luss; and afterwards he espoused Elizabeth, daughter of David Barclay of Ladyland. By the first he had Malcolm his son and heir; and, of the last, he had William, author of that branch of the Crawfurds of Knightswood. He had, moreover, four daughters; viz. Marion, married to John Boyle of Kelburn, of whom the Right Honourable David Earl of Glasgow is lineally descended; Margaret, to James Galbraith of Kilcroich, an ancient family in Stirlingshire; Catherine, to William Wallace of Elderly; Elizabeth, to David Brady of Castletoun in Clackmannanshire. He deceased in the year 1576, and had for his successor, Malcolm his son and heir; who wedded Margaret, daughter of John Cunninghame of Glengarnock, by whom he had John his son and heir, and a daughter, Anne, married to William Cunninghame of Leglan; which Malcolm deceased anno 1595: to whom succeeded John, his son, who departed this life anno 1622, leaving issue, by Margaret his wife, daughter of John Blair of that ilk, John his successor; Malcolm of Newtoun, and James of Knightswood; and a daughter Margaret, married to Hugh Kennedy of Ardmillan.

"To John, last mentioned, succeeded John his son; who married Mary daughter of James Earl of Glencairn, by whom he had John his son and heir; and daughters, Anne, married to Alexander Cunninghame of Corsehill, and had issue; Margaret, to Colonel William Crawford, elder brother to Thomas Crawfurd of Carse, sans issue; and departed this life in November 1629, his estate descending on John his son.

"Which John did, in a very singular manner, distinguish himself in his loyalty to King Charles the First; in consideration whereof His Majesty was pleased to confer on him the dignity of Baronet, in the year 1642; he deceast in Edinburgh in the year 1661, and his corpse were transported to Kilbirny and buried among his ancestors. He was twice married; first, with Margaret, daughter of Robert Lord Burleigh, and, secondly, to Magdalen daughter of David Lord Carnegie, son and heir to David first Earl of Southesk, by whom he had two daughters; Anne, married to Sir Archibald Stewart of Blackhall, and had issue; the second, Margaret, on whom he settled his estate, and to the heirs of her body, obliging them to carry the sirname of Crawfurd, with the Arms of his family; which Margaret took to husband Mr. Patrick Lindsay, second son of John Earl of Crawfurd, by whom she had issue, three sons and as many daughters; viz. John Crawfurd of Kilbirny her son and heir; the second, Patrick; third, Captain Archibald; and daughters, Margaret, married to David, Earl of Glasgow, and had issue; the second, Anne, to Mr. Hary Maule, only brother of James Earl of Panmure, and hath issue; third, Magdalen, to George Dundas of Duddiestoun, and hath issue. Dame Margaret Crawfurd, Lady Kilbirny, died in the month of October 1680.

"To whom succeeded John her son and heir, who was created into the dignity of Viscount of Garnock, Lord Kilbirny, Kingsburn and Drumray, by Her Majesty Queen Anne, by letters patent, bearing date, at Whitehall, the 10th of April 1703: he deceased upon the 24th of December 1708; leaving issue by Margaret, his wife, daughter to James Earl of Bute, Patrick now Viscount of Garnock, his son and heir, whose armorial bearing is two Coats quarterly; 1st, Gules, a Fess, Ermine; 2nd, Azure, a Cheveron, betwixt three Cross patees or supported by two Greyhounds and Crest; an Ermine, Motto 'Sine labe nota.'

"Dame Margaret Crawfurd, Lady Kilbirny, with consent of Lady Kilbirny, with consent of her husband, in the year 1669, alienate the Barony of Easter Greenock to Sir John Shaw of Greenock.

"A quarter of a mile west from the Castle of Easter Greenock, at the east end of a large bay, stands the town of Crawfurdsdike, built of one street, with a convenient harbour, capable to contain ships of a considerable burden. It was erected into a Burgh of Barony, with the privilege of a weekly market and several fairs, in favour of Thomas Crawfurd of Cartsburn, by a Charter from King Charles II. dated the 16th of July, an. 1669. The town is chiefly inhabited by seamen and mechanicks.

"A little towards the south of Crawfurdsdyke, stands the house of Cartsburn, well planted, the principal messuage of that Barony and the seat of Thomas Crawfurd of Cartsburn. which lands were anciently a part of the Barony of Kilbirny, and became the patrimony of a younger brother of that ancient family (in the reign of Queen Mary, whose posterity ended in the person of David Crawfurd of Cartsburn, in the reign of King Charles the I. So the lands came to Malcolm Crawfurd of Newtown, a son of the family of Kilbirny, and acquired from his heirs, an. 1657, by Sir John Crawfurd of Kilbirny. And in the year 1669, disponed by Dame Margaret Crawfurd, Lady Kilbirny, with consent of her husband, to Thomas Crawfurd her cousin, second son of Cornelius Crawfurd of Jordanhill (by Mary his wife, daughter of Sir James Lochart of Lee), lineally descended by Captain Thomas Crawfurd, younger son of Laurence Crawford of Kilbirny. Which Thomas deceased the 15th October 1695, leaving issue, by Jean his wife, daughter of Andrew Semple, son and heir of Robert Semple of Milnbank, Thomas Crawfurd, now of Cartsburn, his son and heir; who hath married Bethia, daughter of Mr. Archibald Robertoun of Bedlay, by whom he has issue, Thomas his son and apparent heir.

"His Armorial bearing is Gules, a Fess, Ermine, betwixt a Crescent in chief and two Swords saltyre-ways, hilted and promel'd or, in Base for Crest, with a Balance, with this Motto, 'Quod tibi hoc alteri.'

"Above the town, on an eminence, stands the castle of Greenock, which overlooks it, surrounded with pleasant parks and enclosures, having on all sides a great deal of beautiful planting, with spacious avenues and terrasses. The Barony of Greenock, as I noticed before, pertained to the Galbraith's of old, and by daughter and co-heiress of Malcolm Galbraith of Greenock, by marriage, came to the family of Shaw of Sauchie, whose ancestor, according to the famous antiquary of Sir George Mackenzie, was descended of Shiach, a son of MacDuff Earl of Fife; and that his descendents took sirname from the proper name of their predecessor, when fixed sirnames came to be used.

"In the Register of the Abby of Pasly, frequent mention is made of the sirname of Shaw. In the reign of King Alexander III. John de Shaw was a witness to that donation, which John, the son of Reginald, made of the lands of Auldhouse to the Monks of Pasly, in the year 1284.

"Thus the family of Sauchie became possess'd of the Barony of Wester Greenock, by marriage of one of the co-heirs of Galbraith of Greenock, in the reign of King Robert the III. After which they were promiscuously design'd of Sauchie and Greenock. For authority of this I have seen a grant by Andrew Abbot of Dunfermline, of the lands of Gartinker, to James Shaw of Greenock, in the year 1439. The lands of Greenock continued in the family of Sauchie until the reign of King James V. that Alexander Shaw of Sauchie gave the lands of Greenock in patrimony to John Shaw his eldest son, by Elizabeth his second wife, daughter of William Cunninghame of Glengarnock. And since the death of George Shaw of Sauchie, without succession, his estate descended to the family of Greenock, who is now the chief of that name and representative of that ancient family. John Shaw, Greenock's ancestor, built the church after the baronies of Easter and Wester Greenock were dissolved from the Paroch of Inverkip and erected into a distinct Paroch, which is ratified by an Act of Parliament in the year 1592. He married in an. 1565 Jean, daughter of John Cunninghame of Glengarnock, his uncle, by whom he had five sons and as many daughters: first, Alexander, who died without succession; the second, James, his successor; the third, Mr. William of Spangow; the fourth, Patrick of Kelsoland; the fifth, Robert, author of that branch of the Shaws of Ganoway in Ireland. His daughters were Elizabeth Montgomery of Braidstane, and Lord Viscount of Airds in the Kingdom of Ireland, ancestor to the Earl Mount-Alexander in that kingdom; Isobel married John Lindsay of the family of Dunrod; Marion married... Campbel of Dovecoathall; Christian married Patrick Montgomery of Craigbouie Esquire; Giles married James Crawfurd of Flattertoun. He departed this life an. 1593.

"To whom succeeded James his son and heir, who wedded Margaret, daughter of Hugh Montgomery of Haslehead, and departing this life in the year 1620, as appears from the probate of his testament yet extant, left issue by the said Margaret his wife, John his only son and heir, who rais'd his fortune considerably and died in the year 1679 leaving issue by Helen his wife, daughter of John Houston of that ilk, John his son and heir; and a daughter, Margaret, married Alexander, Lord Blantyre, and had issue. Which John, during the late usurpation, did engage in the royal cause, and when His Majesty King Charles the II. marched with his army into England, an. 1651, he was constitute Lieutenant Colonel to the regiment of horse commanded by the Earl of Dunfermling; and, at the battle of Worcester, which fell out the third day of September that year, betwixt His Majesty's army and the army of the Rump, under the command of Cromwel and Lambert, the said John did, in a most signal manner, manifest his valour and loyalty to his Sovereign, of which His Majesty was so fully sensible that, as a token of his royal favour, he was pleased to confer on him the honour of Knighthood; and when he obtained the hereditary honour of Baronet from King James VII. by his Patent dated at Windsor, June 28th, 1687, his services to King Charles the II. and his zeal for the interest of the Crown are particularly mentioned as the causes of bestowing that dignity. He married Jean, daughter of Sir William Mure of Rouallan, by whom he had Sir John his son and heir, and several daughters; married Patrick M'Dowal of Logan, and had issue; Sarah to Sir Robert Dickson of Inveresk sans issue; Ann to Tobias Smollet of Bonhill, and had issue.

"Which Sir John died, an. 1694, at Edinburgh, and was buried at the Abby Church or Holyrood-house, his estate and honours devolving on Sir John his son and heir, who departed this life at Edinburgh, an. 1702, and was buried at Greenock among his ancestors, leaving issue by Eleonor his wife, daughter and one of the co-heirs of Sir Thomas Nicholson of Carnock, Sir John his son and heir, and hath married Margaret, daughter of Sir Hugh Dalrymple of North Berwick, Lord President of the College of Justice, by whom he has one daughter, Marion."

This Sir John Shaw represented Renfrewshire in the first Parliament of Great Britain, and in the rebellion in 1715 was distinguished by a vigorous defence of the existing government. On his marriage in 1700 with Margaret Dalrymple, his father and he concurred in making an entail of the estate of Greenock, which they settled on the heirs male of that marriage, which failing on the heirs male of Margaret Shaw, afterwards Lady Houston, the elder Sir John's only daughter.

Sir John Shaw, the younger, as above mentioned, had an only child, Marion, who became wife of Lord Cathcart, and it was in virtue of certain feus made by Sir John in favour of this lady and her husband that that noble family came to have property in the town of Greenock.

Sir John Shaw, the younger, dying without heirs male, the succession to the estates of Greenock devolved upon the descendants of this marriage came to represent the ancient families of Houston, as well as Shaw of Greenock and Nicolson of Carnock. This Sir Michael had three sons, viz.: 1st, The late Sir John Shaw Stewart of Greenock, who in the year 1752, in consequence of his grand-uncle, Sir John Shaw, the younger, succeeded to the estate of Greenock in right of his grandmother, the before-mentioned Dame Margaret Shaw; 2nd, Houston, who, in the same year, succeeded to the entailed estate of Carnock on the death of his grand-uncle Sir John Houston, Bart. (it being a condition in the entail of that estate that it should not be united to the estate of Greenock); 3rd, Archibald, who purchased an estate in Tobago, 1770, and was killed in 1779, from the following occurrence: in the beginning of that year a part of the crew of an American privateer, amounting to fifty men, landed in that island and burnt two plantations, when this gentleman immediately marched against them with a few men of his own company of militia, who happened to be at hand, and bravely attacked them and gave them his fire, but was afterwards unfortunately shot himself and died in a few hours.

Sir Michael had also two daughters: 1st, Margaret, who, in 1764, married Sir William Maxwell of Springkell, Bart, to whom she had four sons, three of whom died unmarried during their father's lifetime, and the fourth, Sir John Heron Maxwell, succeeded to his father and married Stuart-Mary, daughter and heiress of Patrick Heron of Heron, Esq., by whom he has issue. She had also two daughters: 1st, Helenora, married to Claud Alexander of Ballochmyle, Esq., to whom she has three sons and four daughters; 2nd, Catherine, married to her cousin, Michael Stuart Nicolson of Carnock, of whom hereafter. This daughter of Sir Michael's, Lady Maxwell, died in March, 1816, at the advanced age of 74. His second daughter, Helenora, died young. He was succeeded by his eldest son, Sir John Shaw Stewart of Greenock and Blackhall, the fourth Baronet. He was elected member of Parliament for the County of Renfrew in 1780, and again in 1786 and 1790. He was remarkable for a powerful and enlarged understanding, for an independent mind, for the most generous spirit and the most benevolent dispositions; above all, for the most stern and inflexible integrity. His sentiments led him to support the principles of that great statesman, Mr. Fox, with whom, and other illustrious characters of his time, he was in habits of intimacy and friendship. He formed his opinions in politics, as on every other subject, with moderation and candour, but he adhered to them on all occasions with the strictest consistency, and acted up to them with undeviating firmness. The improvements he executed at Ardgowan were upon the most extensive scale, and are highly beneficial as well as beautiful in their effect. He built an excellent house in the modern style, which he surrounded with an extensive park, and the gardens, pleasure grounds, and ample plantations which he planned afford striking proofs of the excellency of his taste. The old tower of

Ardgowan, which formed a part of the ancient mansion, still remains. It is an object beautifully picturesque and rendered peculiarly interesting from having been the gift, along with the ground on which it stands, in 1404, of Robert III. to his son, the direct ancestor of this ancient family. He married Dame Frances Colquhoun, relict of Sir James Maxwell Pollok, but had no issue. He died at Ardgowan August 7, 1812, and was succeeded by his nephew, the late Sir Michael Shaw Stewart, of Greenock and Blackhall, son of his second brother, Houston. He married on the 24th September, 1787, his cousin, Catherine, youngest daughter of Sir William Maxwell of Springkell, Bart., by whom he had issue:—1. Michael Stewart Nicolson (who succeeded to the title and estate on the death of his father, 4th August, 1825); 2. William, who died in infancy; 3. Houston, a captain, R.N.; 4. John Shaw, advocate; 5. Patrick Maxwell, merchant, London; 6. William Maxwell: also three daughters—1. Margaret; 2. Catherine; and 3. Helenora. We have said that the present Sir Michael Shaw Stewart, Bart., M.P., succeeded his father 4th August, 1825. He married 16th September, 1819, Eliza Mary, only daughter of Robert Farquhar, Esq., of Newark, by whom he has had issue; three daughters, Jane, Catherine, and Eliza, and a son, Michael Robert.

The armorial bearing of the Shaws of Greenock is azure, three covered cups, or supported by two savages wreathed about the middle; and for crest a demi savage, with this motto "I mean well."

The armorial bearing of the Blackhal family is or, over a fess cheque azure and argent, a lion rampant gules armed and languid azure; for crest, a lion's head, erazed gules, with this motto, "Spero Meliora."

West from the Barony of Greenock lie the lands of Finnart, a part of the patrimony of the great and noble family of Douglas, which, upon their forfaulture in an. 1445, came by a gift of King

James II. to James first Earl of Arran, an. 1457. and were given, in the year 1510, in patrimony to James Hamilton, his natural son to Mary Boyd, a daughter of Boyd, of Bonshaw. He was legitimate in the year 1512, and in the reign of King James V. was Lord High Treasurer of Scotland, and in the latter end of that King's reign forfaulted in an. 1540 and his estate annexed to the Crown; and the lands of Finnart were bestowed by King James V. upon Alexander Shaw of Sauchie, who, in 1542, disponed Finnart, with the Barony of Wester Greenock, to John Shaw, his son.

*   *   *   *   *

Chapter 2.
PLACES OF WORSHIP.

THE town is situated on the south bank of the Clyde, and in the lower ward of Renfrewshire, in long. 4. 45. 30. W. and lat. 55. 57. 2. W. It is distant about twenty-two miles from Glasgow, has in front an extensive and beautiful bay, which was known by the name of the Bay of St. Lawrence from a small chapel which was dedicated to that Saint and stood on the site of that house at the west corner of Virginia Street belonging to the heirs of the late Mr. Roger Stewart. In digging the foundation of this house a number of human bones were found, which proves that a burying ground must have been attached to it. About 1670 the chapel was in high preservation.

A little below Kilblain stood the remains of a Catholic Chapel, and the tenant was permitted to remove the stones to enclose his garden, in doing which a variety of old coins were found and more particularly the Cruikstone dollar.

A third stood at the extremity of what is now the east boundary of the East Parish, which must have been the principal cemetery, for when the late Mr. King took in these grounds as a kitchen garden many grave stones were found sunk beneath a spade deep. What confirms the authenticity is the fact of this being part of the farm of Chapelton on the estate of Greenock.

These chapels are supposed to have been swept away amidst the general wreck of religious houses at the Reformation, and the inhabitants of the Barony of Greenock were obliged to travel on the Sabbath six weary miles, through bad roads and over dangerous rivulets, to the church of Innerkip, or as it was anciently known as the parish of Daff. Much inconvenience having been found from the great distance of the parish church, John Schaw of Grenok obtained, in 1589, a charter from the King authorising him to build a church for the accommodation of the tenants and inhabitants of his lands of Greenock, Finnart, and Spangock. The following is a copy of the royal charter, granted by King James VI. to Sir John Schaw, for disjoining or separating a particular portion or territory from the parish of Innerkip (which as being the "Mother Church" of the district is still known by the appellation of the "Auld Kirk") for the formation of the parish of Greenock, since divided into three parishes—the West, the Middle or New, and the East Parish. The document which we allude to is dated at Holyrood House, the 18th day of November, 1589, and was subsequently ratified in the Scottish Parliament in 1592, and is as follows:—

"JAMES Be the grace of god king of Scotts To or collectors and vthers vnder ressaveris of the stentis taxationis, subsydis and impositionis ordiner and extraordinar to be raisit and imposit within this realme and all or officeris executors of ony or vther lrez to be direct thairvpon lieges and subdites quhome it efferis quhais knawlege thir or lrez sail cum gretin WIT YE WS being movit wt the ernest zeill and grite affection or louit Johnne schaw of grenok hes ay had to goddis glorie and propagatioun of the trew religioun sen the first professing of the same within or realme And that he continewing in that godlie mynd and gude intentioun upon sindrie ressounable considerationis moving him of conscience and reuerence he beiris to goddis Name Is willing not only on his awin coist to Erect and big one parroche kirk vpon his awin heretage Bot also to appoynt and designne mans and gaird to the samyn wt the haul profiitte and comoditie he hes of teind belanging to the kirk for the help and supporte of the sustentatioun of ane minister thairat Sua that the puir pepill duelling vpoun his lands and heretage qlkis ar all fischers and of a ressounable nowmer duelland four myles fra thair parroche kirk and having ane greit river to pas over to the samyn May haif ane ease in winter seasoun and better comoditie to convene to goddis sruice on the sabboth day and rest according to goddis institution Beand weill allowit of to proceid in the samyn werk baith be the generall assemblie of the kirk and synodall assem. blie of the provine qrin he remanis And we vnderstanding that the accomplisheing of the said godlie and gude wark Will be large coist and expense and grite panes and travellis to the said Johnne and his tenetis THAIRFOIR that thai fasche not nor be hinderit thairin bot rather be encourageit and haif gude occasioun to performe the samyn WE efter or lauchfuil and perfyte aige of Tuentie ane yers compleit and generall revocatioun maid in or parliament Haif gevin grant!t and comittit and be thir or lrez gevis grantis and comittis to the said Johnne schaw of Grenok Oure full power speciall libertie facultie and licence To erect and big the said kirk and designne mans and gaird thairto In and vpoun ony pairt or place within the bounds of his awin lands and heretage quhair he sall think maist comodious and convenient quhairat his haill tenentis salbe haldin to convene to heir goddis worde and Ressaue the sacramentis in all tyme coming and ordanis the samyn to be callit the parroche kirk of grenok And thairfor exeme him his airis and tennentis of his lands and heretage now had and to be had be him and thame fra all keping and convening to their auld parroche kirk in ony tymes cuming Bot at thair awin will and plesr be thir or lrez And declairis thame to be frie and perpetuallie exonerit and dischairgit of all charge and burding of the samyn in stent taxatioun bigging butting or ony vther manner of way in tyme coming And forder vpoun the cause and considerationis foirsaidis we erneistlie willing the said Johnnes godlie intentioun foirsaid and being of guid mynd to move him thairto and recompance him for the samyn Be the tennor of thir or lrez Exemis the said Johnne his airis and tennentis pot and to cum duelling vpoun his proper lands and heretage of grenok fynnartie and spangok with thair pertinentis extending all to twenty aucht pund xiij s worth of land of auld extent lyand within the parochin of Innerkipe and or srefdome of Renfrew ftra all payment of ony pairt of orgy taxatioun stent subside charge and impositioun gtsumeuir to be raisit or imposit within this realme in ony tymes heirefter ather ordiner or extraordiner for ony caus or occasioun that may happin, &c. &c. Gevin vnder or privie seill AT halyruidhous the auchtene day of Nouember The yeir of god Jm vc fourscoir nine yeiris And of or Regnne the twentie thrie yeir per aignat-uram manibus S D N Regis ac cancellarij subscript."

The proprietor having obtained this charter erected a church and manse in 1591, and also set apart a piece of ground adjoining as a churchyard; on the 4th April, 1592, the Synod of Glasgow authorised the burying of the dead in the new kirkyard of Greenock.[1] In 1594 another Act of Parliament was passed in favour of John Shaw, by which his lands of Greenock, Finnart, and Spangock, with all their titles and ecclesiastical duties, were disjoined from Innerkip, and erected into a distinct parsonage and vicarage, which were assigned to the newly erected parish of Greenock. On the 16th September, 1600, the Synod of Glasgow ordained that the inhabitants of Over and Nether Greenock should meet in one congregation. The parish of Greenock continued as thus established till 1636, when there was obtained, from the lords commissioners for the plantation of churches, a decree whereby the baronies of Wester and Easter Greenock and various other lands which had belonged to the parish of Innerkip, with a small detached portion of the parish of Houston, were erected into a parish to be called Greenock, and the church formerly erected at Greenock was ordained to be the parochial church of which Shaw of Greenock was the patron.

The church, though finished in 1591, had not a regular pastor till 1602, when John Lang was appointed minister; in 1640, James Taylor; in 1679, Neil Gillies, privately called by the parish; 1688,—Gordon, officially, who continued till 1691, when he returned to his old charge at Inveraray; in 1694, John Stirling from Inchinnan, who in 1701 was admitted Principal of the College of Glasgow; and in 1704, Andrew Turner from Erskine, who died in 1719. In the same year he was succeeded by his son

---

1. The church as now seen is different from what it was at its first erection, and had not the wings containing Sir Michael S. Stewart's and Cartsburn's seat till about seventy years ago, when it was mostly rebuilt, The oldest gravestone still bears date 1675.

David Turner, who died in 1786. In 1786 Alan M'Aulay was appointed. Some, alleged improprieties of behaviour brought him before the Presbytery; they held their meeting in the present Town Hall, and on that occasion the celebrated Mr. Muir, of Hunter's Hill (who was banished for his share in the revolutionary meetings of the friends of the people), appeared on behalf of the church. Mr. M'Aulay died while his case was under consideration, and was succeeded in 1791 by Robert Steel, the present minister. In 1798 the stipend was only £96 in money, and a glebe of six acres worth £30 yearly. The stipend was afterwards augmented to £111 in money, with thirty-two bolls of meal, and by the Act of Parliament in 1801 authorising feu grants of the glebe for building at an average rent of £100 per acre the value of the glebe has been raised to £600 a year, and the whole revenue of the minister is about £800, with thirty-two bolls of meal yearly, constituting it one of the best livings in Scotland.

The West Parish, which still retains the name of the old parish, comprehends the western part of the town and the greater part of the country district. The patronage belongs to Sir Michael Shaw Stewart of Greenock. The church is situated at the east end of the glebe and close by the shore. It stands in the midst of an extensive burying ground, and though there is nothing remarkable in its appearance has still a venerable aspect. It is built nearly in the form of a cross, and has a small belfry on the west side. Here the first bell which was in Greenock is supposed to have been placed, and till within the last forty years it gave a merry chime on marriage occasions or a mournful toll when some worthy was consigned to the dust. This place continued till 1741 the only place of worship, and contains a seat for Sir Michael the lord of the manor, and another for Crawford of Cartsburn, the proprietor of Cartsdyke. There is also a farmers' gallery, and on the opposite side another for seamen, with a ship full rigged suspended from the roof; the rest is appropriated to general sitters. In wandering through the churchyard there is but little to attract the eye which is not common to every burying ground, and Greenock possesses but few illustrious dead over whose graves we would be apt to linger with emotions of regret. Yet here unnoticed and scarcely known is, now "mouldering in silent dust," Highland Mary, the object of Burns' purest and most exalted attachment and the theme of some of his finest effusions. Here also the father of the illustrious James Watt reposes in peace, though not altogether uncommemorated. And here you are reminded of that awful calamity, the sinking of the steamboat Comet, on the 21st of October, 1825, by observing the grave which contains Sir Joseph Radcliffe's servants who perished on that mournful occasion.

> Thus as we move with solemn tread,
> Above those mansions of the dead;
> Time was, like us they life possessed,
> And time shall be when we shall rest.

The increasing population in 1741 rendered it necessary to have more church accommodation than the parish church afforded, and accordingly this year the new parish church was established and a minister ordained for it. This parish is confined entirely to the town, and is known by the designation of the Mid Parish.

At the time the first minister was ordained there was no regular place of worship except a large loft at the Royal Closs,[1] now occupied partly with Bailie Ewing's office, and in the closs[2] adjoining a bell was hung upon triangles for the purpose of warning the people to church. Up to this time Greenock

---

1. The celebrated George Whitfield preached here on the eve of his embarking from Greenock to America, from these words—" Is there no balm in Gilead, is there no physician there."
2. An enCLOSure, courtyard or entrance to a building such as a tene-ment.—GP

possessed no steeple, and the only tell-tale time could boast of

NEW PARISH CHURCH.
Engraved for Weir's History of Greenock.

was a sun dial placed on the western corner of that house on the
north-east corner formed by the intersection of Cross Shore and
Shaw Streets, and which appears from a stone in front to have

been built in 1716 and was one of the four-slated houses which Greenock was possessed of prior to 1720. In 1753, however, the minister of the Mid Parish remonstrated with the magistrates on the unsafe state of the triangles and wished them repaired, but it was thought by the worthy council a more economical plan to erect a "timber steeple" on the town cellars then finished, and to give the inhabitants the benefit of the clock. This was carried into effect almost immediately, and was considered a chef d'oevre in this species of architecture; and well it might, for the aspiring Greenockians had previously nothing to mark the tardiness or speed of time save the sun dial and Rip Van Winkle's clock "the tall trees' shadow on the garden wall."

In the year 1758, Lord Cathcart gave a present of ground for the purpose of building a church, and the town and a number of individuals gave money for its erection. On the 6th of April, 1759, the foundation was laid, and early in 1761 it was pronounced a substantial, safe building, and immediately occupied as a place of worship. It stands in the middle of the square, fronting the Mid Quay, and has a very elegant appearance. The architecture is plain, having a portico with four pillars of the Ionic order. The steeple, which is a beautiful piece of masonry, was not finished till 1787, and though one hundred and forty-six feet high is still less than was originally intended, and is almost a copy from that of St. Martin's in the Fields, London.

This church contains a seat for the Magistrates, and is capable of holding 1500 sitters; on each side of the pulpit are elegant monuments to the memory of Lieut. Colonel Henry Crawford and Captain George Stewart, both natives of Greenock, who fell in defence of their country during the Peninsular War, and were erected by their early friends and companions. Behind the Magistrates' loft is a plain marble slab to the memory of another townsman, William Spence, whose mathematical attainments were of the highest order, and it is intended to erect near the same place an elegant monument to the memory of Quintin Leitch, an amiable and highly gifted individual, who was for six years Magistrate of Greenock, and who saw executed during this short period the greatest improvements which Greenock can boast of. When the Mid Parish was first disjoined in 1741 James Shaw was ordained minister, in 1771 John Adam from West Kilbride, and in 1793 John Scott the present clergyman. In 1785 the minister's stipend, including sacramental elements and a free manse, was £111, and in 1629 £295.

The East Parish Church is situated near the Rue-end, above the entrance to Bogle Street; it is a plain building surrounded by trees and a wall; close by it is a manse. Though there is nothing imposing in its outward appearance, it is fitted up with some taste inwardly, and contains an elegant monument on the left hand side of the pulpit erected by Anthony Silviera to the memory of his wife. When built in 1774 it was only a chapel of ease, and the first minister, Peter Miller, performed service till 1776. The same year Archibald Reid was elected, who was transferred to Mauchline in 1792. This year Archibald M'Lauchlane was elected, who was transferred to Dundee in 1805. The chapel was vacant for two years in consequence of the proprietors dividing amongst themselves respecting the election of Mr. Joseph Finlayson and Mr. David Watson, which election was set aside by the Court, and Dr. Gilchrist was nominated by Principal Baird. In 1809 it was converted into a parish church, and Dr. Gilchrist was transferred to Edinburgh in 1825, when the Rev. Mr. Menzies, the present minister, was elected. The salary is £200 annually, with a free manse.

The oldest church not connected with the Establishment was the Old Light Burgher Meeting-house of Cartsdyke, built in the memorable 1745 and re-built in the year 1828. The first minister was Mr. M'Ara, every third Sunday; he was succeeded by Mr. Cook, who went to America; Mr. Ritchieson followed, and was succeeded by Mr. Willis in 1780. The present minister, Mr. Moscript, was placed in 1802.

The Burgher Meeting-house in the Market Street was erected in 1758: previous to its erection the members used to meet for worship in a large green, almost behind the Town Hall buildings, where a tent was kept continually standing. In consequence of the noisy situation of the church and the repairs it required it was abandoned[1] in 1802, when the Burgher Chapel in Innerkip Street was erected. The first minister was the Rev. James Ellis, in connection with Paisley: the year following (1758) it was separated from Paisley and stood vacant till 1761, when Mr. John Buist was ordained: he was followed by the Rev. Mr. Dunn, who was succeeded by the Rev. Mr. Barclay, and is at present without a stated minister. Cost £1122.

In 1791 the Gaelic Chapel was erected. It stands close by the West Burn on a rising ground enclosed with a railing, and though a plain substantial building has rather an imposing appearance. The first minister was the Rev. Kenneth Bayne, who died in 1821 and was succeeded the same year by the Rev. Angus Macbean, present minister. Salary about £250. Cost £1700, and can hold 1600 people.

The Burgher Chapel, Nicholson Street, was built in 1791. The first minister was the Rev. Mr. Jack, succeeded by the present Rev. Mr. Wilson. Stipend £200. Cost £1300, and can hold 1000 sitters.

Tabernacle, Sir Michael Street, built in 1806, when the Rev. Mr. Hercus was appointed. Relief, Sir Michael Street, in 1807, when the Rev. Mr. Auld was appointed. Cost £2200, and can hold

---

1. During the time this place was unsold, and when it was almost the, only unoccupied house in 1809, a ball accidently fired from a frigate in the roads fell there about nine in the morning, and having pene-trated the roof forced out a large stone from the south west corner.

1200 sitters. Methodist, Tobago Street, in 1814. Roman Catholic, in 1815: previous to this they held their meetings for four years in the Star Hall. The first regularly officiating clergyman was the Rev. John Davidson; he died in 1815, and was succeeded by the Rev. John Gordon, present incumbent, who opened the new chapel 24th December, same year.

The Baptist Meeting-house was built in 1821, when the Rev. Mr. Edwards was appointed; since the period of his leaving this place no regular clergyman officiates. These buildings have nothing remarkable in their appearance, and are only characterised by the good taste of those who planned and finished them for affording pleasant accommodation to their Various sitters.

In 1823 Blackhall Street Chapel was finished, from designs by Mr. James Dempster of this town, a young artist of rising eminence. It stands upon a fine open space near the shore, and has a very substantial, imposing appearance. The first clergyman is the present incumbent, the Rev. Nathaniel Morren, Cost £3200, and can hold 1600 sitters.

In 1824 the Episcopal Chapel was finished. It stands upon the north side of Gourock Street, and has a chaste and elegant Gothic front designed by and executed under the superintendence of Mr. Dempster in a manner highly creditable to his abilities. It was consecrated by the Rev. Bishop Sandford on the 30th April, 1825, and shortly after the Rev. William D. Carter entered on the ministerial duties of the chapel. On his being appointed Chaplain to the Hon. East India Company in 1829, the Rev. J. M. Williams was elected, but he never entered upon his duties in consequence of his appointment also as Chaplain in India to the East India Company. The Rev. T. H. Wilkinson was nominated his successor. Cost £2300, and can hold 400 sitters.

Having now gone over the different places of worship in the regular succession in which they appear to have been built, some estimate may be formed from thence of the progress of the town and population from the year 1741 till the present period. Greenock may be said to contain almost all sects and persuasions, and the only class of Christians among us, who have no regular place except a hall, are the professors of Universalist doctrines. In 1817 attempts were made to get a place of worship for the Unitarians, but this failed in consequence of the fewness of their number. The inhabitants have been always considered as a church-going people, and though the accommodation is reckoned no more than sufficient for the population the churches are, with few exceptions, well attended.

The following abstract from the sessional records for the years 1820 and 1828 will be of importance. The Register of Births cannot but be inaccurate from the negligence of parents on this important point. A Register of Deaths has never been kept, but it is intended to commence one immediately.

OLD PARISH.

Marriages in 1820, 124.—In 1828, 128.

Births in 1820, 263—Of which there are males, 145; females, 118. In 1828, 232—Of which there are males, 131; females, 101.

Paupers receiving parochial aid in 1820, 495—of which there were males, 69; females, 327.

Assessment for 1820, £1200—for 1828, £962 6s. 3d.

MID PARISH.

Marriages in 1820, 60.—In 1828, 68.

Births in 1820, 93—Of which there were males, 51; females, 42; In 1828, 68—of which there were males, 26; females, 32.

Paupers receiving parochial aid in 1820, 338—of which there were males, 34; females, 304. In 1828, 312—of which there were males, 36. females, 326.

Assessment for 1820, £800—for 1828, £220.

EAST PARISH.

Marriages in 1820, 37.—In 1828, 43.

Births in 1820, 69—Of which there were males, 37; females, 32. In 1828, 90—of which there were males, 48; females, 42.

Paupers receiving parochial aid in 1820, 207—of which there were males, 68; females, 139. In 1828, 106—of which there were males, 22; females, 84.

Assessment for 1820, £450—for 1828, £220.

The following sums have been considered necessary for 1829; Old Parish, £830; New Parish, £700; East Parish, £200; Fancy Farm, £190.

We have only noticed one burying ground as belonging to the town, but the crowded state of this old receptacle of our fathers' ashes rendered it necessary in 1789 to feu a large piece of ground at the top of Innerkip Street, which was enclosed with a wall, and this was still further augmented by feuing an additional field in 1816, which is also surrounded by a wall having a centre range which divides both places.

*　　*　　*　　*　　*

Chapter 3.
SCHOOLS & EDUCATION.

SCOTLAND has been long famed for its attention to the education of the rising race, and Greenock has been by no means behind in this important subject: The benefit of Parochial Schools has been long felt and acknowledged, and the reason why there is none here has been matter of wonder to many. A correspondent in the Greenock paper for April 12, 1809, has the following remarks:— "Can any of your intelligent correspondents inform me why no such establishment as a Parochial School has existed in Greenock for nearly 40 years past? and on what grounds the rising generation in this place are deprived of such an institution." Notwithstanding of this want, Greenock has produced some who have been an ornament to their country. Witness the never-dying name of James Watt; in Mathematics, William Spence; and in the lighter and more amusing parts of literature, John Galt. There are few indeed but must have felt the force of Lord Eldon's handsome compliment when presenting the Greenock petition against the Catholic claims, amounting to nearly five thousand signatures, when he observed— "that this was a proof of education in Scotland, and in particular of Greenock, that in a petition so numerously signed the signatures were all well written, and only three marks." In further proof of this, Greenock has sent forth enterprising and intelligent merchants to almost every mercantile depot in the world; and as every person has a wish to know the school boy scenes of other days,

> "Where in his noisy mansion skilled to rule,
> The village master taught his little school,"

was appointed to inquire into the expense of such an establishment, and on the 22nd of December they gave in their report, with we subjoin the following interesting remarks from the pen of George Williamson, Esq.:—

"Mr. Robert Arrol, the author of an elegant translation of Cornelius Nepos[1] published in 1774, with a vocabulary, chronological table, and erudite notes, was the first master of the Grammar School of Greenock. He also published translations of Eutropius,[2] and select colloquies of Erasmus—but what most distinguishes him is the circumstance of his having been one of the preceptors of the immortal James Watt. Mr. John Marr was Mr. Watt's instructor in Mathematics. It is regretted that nothing further of Mr. Marr is known, excepting that it appears from the records of the society of Free Masons, known by the appellation of the 'Greenock Kilwinning, No. 11,' of which he was a member, that he was of Glasgow, at all events that he was initiated in the mysteries of the craft in that city.

The old Tenement at the foot and on the west side of Smith's Lane, otherwise known as the 'Wee Kirk Street,' where it joins the Vennel, is the house in which the Town Schools were kept at the period alluded to, and probably belonged to some one of the Magistrates of the day.

"On the 2nd October, 1751, Mr. John Woodrow was appointed Grammar Schoolmaster on the decease of Mr. Arrol. To this office he united that of Session Clerk. It is not known when he died, but his successor's name was Mr. Bradfute, who continued in office for about four years, and on his death or resig-

---

1. Cornelius Nepos was a Roman author of biographical and historical works.—GP
2. Eutropius was a Roman historian whose 10 volume work provides details of the British campaigns by Caesar and others. His work was used by Jerome, the biblical scholar, writing in the 5th century.—GP

nation—for I have heard he removed to the Grammar School of
Glasgow—was on the 15th October, 1769, succeeded by Mr.
John Wilson.[1] This respectable individual was the author of
"Clyde," an elegant poem republished at Edinburgh in 1803. A
very spirited biographical sketch is prefixed to it by the late Dr.
Leyden, from which, however, I cannot forbear to make the
following quotation, as illustrative of the state of Greenock as
regarded statistics and learning sixty years ago.

"I have now (says Dr. Leyden) to relate a singular transaction, which
I can scarcely believe would have taken place in any district of Scotland
but the west, so late as the 1767. Greenock at this period was a thriving
seaport, rapidly emerging into notice. In the beginning of last century it
consisted of a single row of thatched houses stretching along a bay
without any harbour. In 1707 a harbour began to be constructed, but the
town increased so slowly that in 1755 its population amounted only to
about 3800 souls. About the latter period, however, it began to increase
rapidly, and continued to flourish till the commencement of the American war. Still, however, its inhabitants were more remarkable for
opulence and commercial spirit than for their attention to literature and
science. During the struggle between Prelacy and Presbytery in
Scotland, Greenock, like most of the towns and districts in the west of
Scotland, had imbibed the most intolerant spirit of Presbyterianism; a
spirit which at no period had been favourable to the exertions of poetical
fancy, and which spent the last efforts of its virulence on the Douglas of
Home. Induced by this religious spirit, and by a cool mercantile attention to prudence, the Magistrates and Minister of Greenock, before they
admitted Mr. Wilson to the superintendence of the Grammar School,
stipulated that he should abandon '*the profane and unprofitable art of
poem-making.*' To avoid the temptation of violating this promise, which
he esteemed sacred, he took an early opportunity of committing to the

---

1.   John Wilson (1720-1789) is the subject of a poem written by Doug-
     las Dunn: 'John Wilson in Greenock'. (St. Kilda's Parliament, Faber
     1981.)—GP

flames the greater part of his unfinished manuscripts. After this he never ventured to touch his forbidden lyre, though he often regarded it with that mournful solemnity, which the harshness of dependance and the memory of its departed sounds could not inspire.

"He seems during life to have considered this as the crisis of his fate, which condemned him to obscurity, and sometimes alluded to it with acrimony. In a letter to his son George, attending the University of Glasgow, dated Jan. 21, 1779, he says—'I once thought to live by the breath of fame; but how miserably was I disappointed when, instead of having my performance applauded in crowded theatres, and being caressed by the great—for what will not the Poetaster, in his intoxicating delirium of possession, dream I was condemned to bawl myself to hoarseness to wayward brats, to cultivate sand and wash Ethiopians, for all the dreary days of an obscure life, the contempt of shopkeepers and brutish skippers.' "

"Cruel as was the sacrifice which Mr. Wilson was thus compelled to make of the offspring of his imagination at the shrine of prejudice, yet let it not be supposed that the soil became unproductive of the flowers of literature under such blighting influence, or that poetry has been uncultivated in Greenock since his day."

"Mr. Wilson died 2nd June, 1789, having two years previously been compelled to retire from the labours of his office by reason of the growing infirmities of age and a worn out constitution. "Mr. Wilson was succeeded by Mr. Thomson, who remained in office down to 29th October, 1794, when Mr. Daniel M'Farlane was appointed his successor, and for the long period of thirty years continued to maintain the reputation which the Greenock Grammar School had acquired under his predecessor."

"Mr. M'Farlane was succeeded on his resignation in 1822 by Mr. Potter, a young gentleman of learning and talents, united to the most unassuming modesty, and who, had he been spared to see long life, would have added another to the number of a class

of men to whom the community of Greenock owe a debt of gratitude."

"On Mr. Potter's death, the present incumbent Mr. Brown was
appointed his successor; of him, of course, I am precluded from
saying anything farther than to express an earnest hope that the
youth of Greenock shall long enjoy the advantages of the tuition
of so able, zealous, and successful teacher."

When the Mid Parish Church was finished, the Town Schools
removed to the loft at Royal Closs, and continued there, with their
various teachers, till about the year 1806. The first teacher of the
English School was John M'Adam; he resigned in 1772, and was
succeeded by John Irvine. On Mr. Irvine's resignation in 1779,
Hugh Mitchell was appointed, who was the last teacher that
received a salary from the town.

In 1772 Robert Nicol was appointed Master of the Mathematical School. In 1775 Captain Campbell, of the Prince of Wales,
Revenue Cruiser, made a present to the town of an Azimuth
compass, which was placed under Mr. Nicol's charge, and was
the first of this valuable instrument ever seen in Greenock. In
1781 Mr. Lamont was appointed, and continued in the situation
till 1827, when he was succeeded by Mr. Robson, the present
master.

Till 1774 the Schools were entirely under the control of the
Magistrates and Town Council, but the increasing population
brought a number of talented individuals about this time, who
taught with great success. In 1806 the Academy was built, and
since that period has continued under the charge of its highly
respectable master, C. Buchanan.

At present the Schools are numerous. There is a Free School
situated in Ann Street, which is kept up by voluntary subscription
and educates annually about 600 poor children; and there is an
Infant School, established in 1828, on Mr. Wilderspin's plan.
Independent of these the following teachers may be mentioned:—

The Messrs. White, English, Writing, etc., George's Square; Mr. Hunter, English, and Mr. Nicol, Writing, Sir Michael Street; Mr. Murray, English, Academy Buildings; Mr. Anderson, English, Rue-end; the Rev. Mr. Robertson, Boarding School, Glebe, where all the branches of education are taught. Besides those now enumerated there are a number of other schools, and, though last not least, there is a Female School of Industry which has done much good, and has been superintended by young ladies whose exertions in the cause of the less fortunate of their sex is beyond all praise.[1]

Though the education, in connection with mercantile and other useful pursuits, has been attended to with much care, yet schools of a different order have not been neglected. Sabbath Evening Schools are to be found in every district of the town, and the good which has resulted from this gratuitous teaching has been felt and acknowledged. The Old Parish has schools under the charge of the Session, and the Mid and East Parish have similar establishments. The Relief and Burgher congregations allow the children to meet for an hour after divine service in the afternoon, and they are taught, as in other schools, from the Scriptures, Shorter Catechism, and other approved works for the instruction of the young.

The Town Hall and Public Offices are situated in Hamilton Street. They were planned by James Watt in 1765, and finished the following year. In order to have the benefit of the Hall for their meetings, the Lodge, Greenock Mountstuart Kilwinning, No. 11, advanced £50 to assist in the building. This building has

---

1. In 1779, an honest Frenchman made his appearance in town for the purpose of teaching dancing. He petitioned the Magistrates and Town Council to get the loft at Royal Closs after teaching hours but was refused, lest the "tripping on the fantastic toe "might injure the cellars and bring the town into unnecessary expenses.

been altered since its first erection, having had on the ground
floor, where are now shops, a prison and the Council Chambers,
In front of both of those used to be placed four field-pieces made
of brass, and here a sentinel paraded in consequence of the
Guard-house being then immediately behind. This place has been
for some time used as the Police Office, and its immediate vicinity to the Court Hall makes it very convenient. In the Hall, which
is spacious, there are two excellent paintings of King George the
Third and his Queen. The rest of the apartments are occupied by
the Town Clerk, Procurator-Fiscal, and the Town Treasurer.

Previous to the erection of this building, and in 1753, the
Magistrates and Council met in a shade[1] in William Street, where
Messrs. Macfie, Lindsay & Co.'s grocery is situated: here also the
first postoffice was kept, and the fire-engine, which arrived in
Greenock in 1753, was placed under the charge of a superintendent with a salary of 30s. annually. It is to be regretted that the
council records go no farther back than 1749, the early part of this
chronicle having been torn out by some sacrilegious hand. It
bears entire, however, the following liberal Charter, granted by
Sir John Schaw in 1751:—

"SIR JOHN SCHAW of GREENOCK, Barronet Baron of the Barrony
of Greenock and Burgh of Barrony thereof, to ALL AND SUNDRY to
whom these Presents shall come, GREETING;

"WHEREAS, by several Charters under the Great Seal, the Town is
Erected into a Burgh of Barony, with the same liberties, priviledges, and
jurisdictions granted to, or used and exercised by, any other Burgh of
Barony within Scotland. And, Whereas, I, by my Chatter, bearing date
the thirtieth day of January, one thousand seven hundred and forty-one,
granted power to the Fewars and Subfewars of the said Burgh of Barony
to meet yearly and choise Managers of the Publick Funds of the said
Town, arising from a voluntary Assessment laid on themselves upon all

---

1. A shed or roofed structure.—GP

Malt grinded by them at my Milns of Westward Greenock. And, Whereas, by an Act passed in the fourth Session of this present Parliament, a duty of two pennies Scots is imposed on the pint of all Ale brewed in the Town of Greenock, and that for repairing the Harbour of Greenock, and other purposes mentioned in the said Act;—and John Alexander, Writer; Robert Donald, Robert Rae, James Warden, Gabriel Mathie, William Gammell, James Watt, and James Butcher, Merchants, and Nathan Wilson, Surgeon, all of the Town of Greenock, are thereby appointed Trustees of the Funds arising from the Paid impost of two pennies on the pint of Ale; and power is thereby given to them to name their successors in office;—which Act commenced upon the first day of June last, and endures for thirty-one years, and to the end of the then next Session of Parliament.

"And I, Considering, That, by the great increase of the said Town and Burgh of Barony, it is now become necessary that the Police and Government thereof should be put under proper regulations, and that there should be a perpetual succession of a competent number of the Inhabitants or Burgesses of the said Burgh of Barony chosen, with Baillies, Treasurer, Clerk, and Officers of Court, for the constant management of the Funds or Common Good of the said Burgh of Barony, administration of Justice, and maintaining Peace and Good Order within the same And also, Considering, That it will tend greatly to the advancement of these purposes, that during the subsistence of the said Act of Parliament, the Trustees thereby appointed, and their successors in office, have the government of the Town and management of the Public Funds thereof—therefore, I do, by these presents, as Baron of the said Barony of Greenock and Burgh of Barony, thereof, Give and Grant full Power, Warrant, and Commission to all the Fewars and Subfewars of the said Town and Burgh of Barony of Greenock, To meet and Convene themselves, upon the second Monday of September current, at Ten of the Clock in the Forenoon; and then and there to make choise of the said Nine Trustees to be Magistrates and Counsellors of the said Burgh; whereof, two to be Baillies, one to be Treasurer, and the other six to be Councellors; With Power to the said Baillies, and their successors in office, in all time coming, after the said second Monday of September current, of holding Courts weekly, and oftener, if necessary, within the said Burgh, for administrating Justice to the Inhabitants therein; of seizing, arresting, imprisoning, and otherwise punishing transgressors and delinquents, conform to the Laws of the Land; of levying escheats, fines, and other amerciaments, and, if necessary, poinding and distrenzaeing therefor; and with power to the said Baillies, Treasurer, and Councellors, and their successors in office, to choise Clerks, Seargeands, Apprizers, and all other necessary Officers and Members of Court; and with power to manage the Funds and Common Good presently belonging, or that, at any time hereafter, shall belong, to the said Town and Burgh of Barony—and that in place of the nine Managers chosen and appointed to be chosen by the said Charter granted by me in the year one thousand seven hundred and forty-one: And, with Power, also, to make Rules, Laws, and Statutes, for the advantage of the Burgh, and maintaining good order and peace within the same; and to put the same to due execution: And, with Power, also, of receiving and admitting Merchants and all kinds of Tradesmen, and others, to be free Burgesses within the said Burgh-no more being to be exacted or demanded than thirty merks Scots for the admission of each Burgess: And, Generally, with Power to the said Baillies, Treasurer, and Councell, to use and exercise all other liberties and priviledges and jurisdictions, in the same manner, and as freely as those of any other Burgh of Barony in Scotland do or may do.

"And, it is hereby Declared, That during the thirty-one years mentioned in the said Act of Parliament, the Treasurer of the said Burgh is to be changed at the end of every two years, and others chosen in their place, who are Trustees, in virtue of the said Act of Parliament for managing the Fund arising from the impost on Ale And after the expiry and termination of the said thirty-one years, the Treasurer and two of the Councellors of the said Burgh are to be removed at the end of every year, and one of the Baillies at the end of every two years; for which purpose, and for choosing a Baillie and Treasurer, and two Councellors, in place of those removed, as above mentioned, the whole Fewars, Subfewars, and Burgesses of the said Burgh, and Burgesses being always actual residenters therein, are hereby empowered, in all time coming, to meet upon the second Monday of September yearly—any Fewar, Subfewar, or Burgess of the said Burgh, being capable, after outrunning of the thirty-one years above mentioned, of being chosen a Baillie, Treasurer, or Councillor: And the method of Election, during the running of the said thirty-one years, is hereby declared and appointed to be by each Fewar, Subfewar, and Burgess present, his giving into the Clerk a list, signed by him, containing the names of the Baillie and Treasurer to be changed, and the names of the Trustees he elects and chooses to be Baillie and Treasurer for the year ensuing: and after outrunning of the said thirty-one years, the method of Election is hereby declared and appointed to be by each Fewar, Subfewar, and Burgess present, his giving into the Clerk a list, signed by him, of the persons to be removed out of the Councell and those he elects and chooses in their place, and mentioning the names of those he chooses to be Baillie and Treasurer; and where votes are equal, the former Baillies, Treasurer, and Councellors, are hereby declared to have the casting vote.

"And, it is also hereby declared, That one of the Baillies, with four of the Councellors, or with the Treasurer and three of the Councellors, shall be a Quorum, invested with the power of executing all and everything hereby committed to the Baillies, Treasurer, and Councellors.

"And it is also declared, That, after outrunning of the said thirty-one years, the Baillies, Treasurer, and Councellors, must, in all time coming, be actual residenters within the town of Greenock, and their non-residence in the said Town shall as effectually disqualify them for any of these offices as if they were naturally dead; without prejudice, nevertheless, upon their returning to be actual residenters in the said Town, of their being re-elected into any of the said offices, during their actual residence, as above mentioned and upon the death or disqualification by non-residence, as above mentioned, of any of the Town Councell of the said Burgh, consisting of the Baillies, Treasurer, and Councellors foresaid, the rest of the Town Councell are hereby empowered to choose another in his place; and that as oft as the said event shall happen, the whole proceedings at Elections, whether by the Town Councell, or by the whole Fewars, Subfewars and Burgesses, being always to be fairly entered and ingrossed in a Book or Books, to be kept by the Clerk for that purpose. And further, it is hereby provided and declared, That if, by any accident or neglect, no Election shall be made at any stated yearly diet for election, or being made, but not duly, shall be set aside, or reduced,—Then, and in either of these cases, and as often as the same shall occur, the whole Fewars, Subfewars, and Burgesses of the said Town and Barony of Greenock, shall have full power and liberty to meet upon and choose two Baillies, a Treasurer, and six Councellors, for the government of the said Town and other purposes, and with the powers above mentioned; and to meet yearly thereafter, upon the said and remove part of them, and choose others in their place, in manner as is above provided such power and liberty being always hereby so quali-fied, that if the necessity of such new election of a whole Town Council happen, during the running of the thirty-one years mentioned in the said Act of Parliament, then the Trustees, for the time executing the said Act of Parliament, are to be chosen the Baillies, Treasurer, and Councellors of the said Burghs: Providing and Declaring always that this Grant is given by me, and accepted by the said Fewars, Subfewars, and Burgesses, with, and tinder this express condition, that the Baron Baillie, or Baillies of me and my heirs, in the Barrony of Greenock, shall have a Cumulative Jurisdiction over the inhabitants of the Town of Greenock, with the Baillies to be chosen, as above mentioned, in virtue of this Grant.

"And, Further, in case this Grant shall, in any point or circumstance, be construed or interpreted in Law to be contrary to the Entail of Green-ock, and my powers with respect to the said Town and Burgh of Barrony, it is hereby expressly Declared, that the same is granted and accepted with this provision and quality, That the same is to be regulated and limited according to the powers I shall be found to have with respect to the said Town and Burgh of Barrony of Greenock, and shall stand and be effectual in so far as consistent therewith; the same being granted, not to exceed but to exerce my powers, for the good and advantage of the said Town and Burgh.

"And also, it is hereby Declared. that this Grant shall be but preju-dice to the said Subfewars and Fewars, their useing the said Charter granted by me to them in the year one thousand seven hundred and forty-one, for the purposes therein mentioned, and that whenever they shall find necessary so to do. And, in case it shall be found necessary, competent, or proper, that this Grant should be compleated by Infeftment, I hereby desire and require you and each of you, conjunctly and severally, my Baillies in that part, hereby specially constitute, That, incontinent after sight hereof, ye pass and give Heritable State and Seasine, Actual Real, and Corporal possession of All and Whole, the Powers, Liberties, Priviledges, and Jurisdictions, above mentioned, to the Baillies, Treasurer, and Councellors of the said Burgh of Barrony of Greenock, and their successors in office; and that, by delivering to them or their certain Attorney or Attornies in their names, Bearers hereof of a Book and Baton, and all other symbolls usual and requisite, to be holden of me and my Heirs in the Estate of Greenock, for rendering Justice to the inhabitants of the said Burgh, maintaining Peace and Good Order within the same, and duly manageing their Common Good and Publick Funds; for doing whereof, these presents shall be to you, and each of you, conjunctly and severally, as said is, a full power and warrant, Coy renting to the Registration hereof in the Books of Councell and Session, therein to remain for preservation; and for that. end constitute my Pro'rs: In Witness whereof, I have subscribed these presents, wrote on Stampt Vellum, by James Alison, Clerk to Robert Dalrymple, Writer to the Signet, Att Drummore, in East Lothian, the second day of September, one thousand seven hundred and fifty-one years-before these Witnesses, Hew Dalrymple of Drummore, Esq., one of the Senators of the Colledge of Justice; the said Robert Dalrymple, and the said James Alison, Writer hereof.

(Signed)   "JOHN SCHAW,"

"HEW DALRYMPLE, Witness."
"Ro. DALRYMPLE, Witness."
"JAMES ALISON, Witness."

On the 6th August, 1751, the first Magistrates and Council were elected, and were as follows:—

Bailies: John Alexander, Robert Donald.

Treasurer: James Butcher.

Councillors: W. Gammell, Robert Rae, James Warden, James Watt, Gabriel Mathie, Nathan Wilson,

The first Guard-house was at the foot of Cowgate, and continued till removed to the Town Hall; and the place more recently used for this purpose is situated in the lane leading from the Square to the Green Market.

*   *   *   *   *

Chapter 4.
'GUARDIANS OF THE SICK POOR.'

A Dispensary for the benefit of the Sick Poor was established in 1801. The house appropriated for it was situated in Manse Lane; it was afterwards removed to the ground floor of a house in Cathcart Street, the site of which is occupied with part of the Exchange Buildings. The sum at first subscribed for the establishment of this charity, and for its support for the first year, was £131 3s. From the 1st July, 1801, 177 patients were admitted, and from its commencement, until united with the Hospital in 1809, there were 1715. By the constitution the poor, when sick at home and unable to attend, were visited by one of the surgeons daily, and the medicines prescribed were prepared by an apothecary, who, with the medical attendants, four in number, were elected annually by the subscribers. Surgical instruments, with apparatus used for the recovery of drowned persons, belonged to the Dispensary.

In 1806 a contagious fever became very prevalent, and was traced to the seamen of a prize vessel brought into harbour. The inmates of lodging houses first caught the infection, and from them it soon extended to other families. The alarm was great, but, by means of the Dispensary, much misery was relieved and the progress of the disease finally arrested. On the 23rd of October, 1806, Dr. Spiers, one of the surgeons of the Dispensary, directed the attention of the committee to the establishing an Hospital, or Fever-house, where the poor would be removed from their own uncomfortable dwellings, not only for their own sakes but for the purpose of checking infection. At this meeting a sub-committee one from Dr. Colquhoun, "As to the rise and progress of the Infectious Fever prevailing," and another by Dr. Speirs "On the subject of the present and other Epidemical Diseases." On the 3rd January, 1807, it was resolved that an Hospital or Infirmary be erected, and subscriptions were opened for carrying the object into effect. On the 23rd February the first meeting of subscribers was held in the Tontine, when Alexander Dunlop, Esq., Banker, informed the meeting that Sir John Shaw Stewart had offered forty falls[1] of ground for the site of the building. A plan was submitted by Mr. Aird, Master of Works, and on the 28th September, 1808, Mr. George Dempster's estimate, amounting to £1150, was agreed to. The subscriptions amounted to £2357 11s 7d. It may be worth remarking that many individuals excused themselves from subscribing to this necessary institution by saying "That a Bridewell[2] was more wanted." One of the committee, who was zealous in the cause, and at the same time jocular, would not let them get off with this excuse, but at once said, "both were intended," and for this reason from the subscriptions £500 was set apart for building a Bridewell, which was the foundation of the fund for this erection. At a general meeting on the 3rd May, 1809, rules, &c., were adopted for the management of the charity; office-bearers were appointed, the furniture, etc., removed from the Dispensary, which now merged into that of the Hospital. At the time the house was opened the cost amounted to £1504 7s., and on the 14th June the first patient was admitted. From that period till 1st May, 1810, 51 patients were admitted, and   149   received   benefit   as   out-patients.

The airing-ground being found rather limited. application was made to the late Sir Michael Shaw Stewart for a small addition.

---

1. Unit measurement equal to 18 Scots feet.—GP
2. A bridewell was a house of correction or jail especially for minor offences. [After Bridewell, London.]—GP

He, in the most liberal manner, on looking at the spot, desired his factor to make over to the trustees the whole piece of ground, from the original house to the street, being much more than was asked.

The Hospital, since its establishment, has continued to rise in usefulness, and there is no doubt but it will keep pace, in that respect, with the increase of trade and population. It has been found necessary to extend its accommodation by adding two wings to it, and this will be soon completed at about £900, a sum which was at once cheerfully subscribed and rapidly carried into effect. This must be always considered as the first of public charities in town, and well deserves the support of the public. Much responsibility attaches to the managers, and it is to be trusted that a proper and enlightened feeling will ever actuate them in the discharge of their duty. Their motto ever should be, "We are the *guardians* of the *Sick Poor*."

The appearance of the Hospital, since the additions were made to it, is rather elegant. It is situated on the east side of Innerkip Street, immediately between the burying-ground and Burgher Meeting-house, and if anything is to be regretted, it is its being too much confined to give full effect to a house, simple in its design, but neat and chaste in its execution.

OFFICE-BEARERS FOR THE FIRST YEAR OF THE INFIRMARY.

Chief Magistrate, President.
William Forsyth, Esq., Vice-President.
James Leitch, Treasurer.
Robert Steuart and John Davidson, Secretaries.

Committee of Management.

George Robertson, Chairman.
Duncan M'Naught, Deputy-Chairman.

John Scott, D.D.	James Park.
Robert Steel.	Archibald Baine.
Thomas Ritchie.	James Watt.
John M'Nair, Writer.	William Dingwall.

Medical Attendants.

Andrew Hill, M.D.	John Colquhoun, M.D.
John Speirs, M.D.	Colin Campbell, M.D.

As nearly in connection with the Greenock Hospital, we may state that on the 14th December, 1818, the medical practitioners in town and neighbourhood formed themselves into an Association, the object of which was to promote professional intercourse and improvement. On the 2nd August, 1820, a code of Laws were agreed to for the regulation of the Association. On the 25th September, same year, it was incorporated into a body politic by charter under the name of "The Greenock Medical and Chirurgical[1] Association." The members meet regularly once a month during the winter, and after the private business is finished an essay on some medical subject, composed by one of the members, is read and discussed; a professional question is then proposed and debated, and the essay for next meeting announced. The attention of the members is thus called and directed to important subjects, and different views are elicited, and preconceived opinions either altered or confirmed. The Association holds in its right a Library, which, by the charter, is secured to the Society in all time coming. The Library is supported by a fund arising from

---

1. Archaic word for surgical; a chirurgeon was the then equivalent of a surgeon. [from the Old French cirurgeon.]—GP

entry money and by annual contributions; it is now valuable, and rapidly increasing, and contains at present about 600 volumes. This cannot fail of being highly beneficial to the community, by yielding to the practitioners in medicine and surgery ready access to the acquirement of professional knowledge. There is likewise, under the conservation of the Association, a Museum consisting of anatomical preparations and subjects in natural history. At and since the commencement of the Association there have been admitted 52 members.

The original office-bearers were as follows:—

OFFICE-BEARERS OF THE GREENOCK MEDICAL AND CHIRURGICAL ASSOCIATION IN 1818.

President, ... Dr. Speirs.
Vice-President, ... Dr. Kirk.
Stewards, ... Mr. Wm. Dobson.
. . . . Mr. A. N. Houston.
Secretary, ... Alexander Adam,

OFFICE-BEARERS FOR 1828-9.

President, ... Dr. Speirs.
Vice-President, ... Mr. Campbell, Largs.
Treasurer, ... Dr. Robertson.
Secretary, ... Dr. Mackie.
Librarian, ... Dr. King.
Censors, ... Mr. Turner.
. . . . Mr. Speirs.
Superintendent of Museum, ... Mr. Speirs.
Vaccinator, ... Mr. A. N. Houston.

* * * * *

Chapter 5.
PUBLIC BUILDINGS.

TONTINE.

Engraved for Weir's History of Greenock.

IN 1804, the Tontine, which is a substantial handsome building, was erected. It is situated in Cathcart Street, and contains a large hall, with 12 sitting-rooms and 30 bedrooms. The subscribers, 400 in number, were procured in the course of two days, making the subscription, which was £25 per share, amount to £10,000, In consequence of non-payment 23 were struck off the list, which reduced the members to 377, and at this period about 290 were still on the list.

Nearly opposite is situated the Exchange Buildings, which were finished in 1814, at an expense of £7000. This spacious erection, though rather confined to give it full effect, is a great ornament to the street. It contains two Assembly Rooms, which are fitted up in a splendid manner, and when lighted and decorated and enlivened with the gay assemblage for an evening party has a brilliant appearance. The first assembly took place in Alexander's Land, William Street, afterwards in the Town Hall, Star Hall, Buck's Head Inn, Mason Lodge, and Tontine. In the lower range is a large room occupied as the Coffee Room, which receives a variety of London and provincial papers, besides the periodicals of the day and works giving information on commercial subjects. The expense is defrayed by an annual subscription of 35s., but strangers are admitted without introduction, and are considered as such for six weeks' residence in town. The first Coffee Room was in the low flat of "Wm. Alexander's great tenement of land in William Street," and, if then limited in its dimensions, had one great advantage of bringing the subscribers to a close and friendly reciprocity of sentiment. The present Town Hall was also used for a considerable time for this purpose, and from thence to its present situation the Coffee Room was removed in 1814. The Greenock Bank occupies the western side, and has an extensive business, not only with London and various commercial towns, but also with the Highlands and surrounding neighbourhood. This Bank was established under the firm of Dunlop, Houston & Co. in 1785, and in June of same year their first bank-note was issued. It was at first situated in the land to the westward of the Town Hall; from thence it was removed to the Bank Buildings, West Breast, where it continued till September, 1820. The sunk-storey has been occupied as a wine-cellar, and, from the coolness and easy access to it, is generally well

employed. Behind this building a small neat Theatre was built by
the late Mr. Stephen Kemble. Previous to this erection the lovers
of the drama used to assemble near the Rue-end, in that place
occupied as a counting-room, etc., by Robert Angus, Esq. Here
the Theatre used to be much frequented, but of late years the taste
for this species of entertainment has been much on the decline,
and a full house can rarely be got when even the London stars pay
a visit to the town. This is not peculiar to Greenock alone;
Scotland in general has ceased to bestow its patronage on an
amusement which, by its early records, seems to have been
anything but well received.

The old mansion[1] of the Shaw Stewart family stands upon a
fine rising ground above the Assembly Rooms, and commands a
most extensive view of the Town. This situation, before the buildings encroached upon it, must have been one of delightful retire-
ment and beauty. There must have been various additions built to
the house since its first erection. An ancient well close by bears
date upon it 1629. Over one of the entrances to the garden is
affixed 1635; but the oldest date in connection with the house is
over a back entrance—1637. The front and greater part of the
building is of modern erection, and is said to have been planned
by James Watt. It was here, however, that baronial hospitality
spread the board, and from this place John Shaw, with about 200
of his tenantry, marched to the assistance of King Charles II. and
fought with that prince at the battle of Worcester, 3rd September,
1651. The banner which was carried on this occasion was
preserved till about 1796, and hung along with the Town flags in
the Coffee Room, but since this period was never seen. It was in
consequence of the zeal of John Shaw that he was created a
Baronet under the flag on the field of battle. Sir John was residing

---

1. The family ceased to reside here in 1754, and now occupy the noble
   mansion of Ardgowan.

here in 1715, and on the Duke of Argyle's[1] arrival in Edinburgh on the 14th September he addressed a letter earnestly begging assistance. "From which place and Cartsdyke he was reinforced with somewhat more than 100 men, accompanied by their minister, the Rev. Mr. Turner. These remained under the orders of His Grace for 80 days, doing duty all that time the same as the regular troops. Besides the above that were thus employed abroad, there were 50 men belonging to Greenock and 25 to Cartsdyke who kept watch every night, bringing all the boats from the south side of the Clyde to prevent the rebels, especially Rob Roy and his thieves, from transporting themselves across and plundering the adjacent country." Again in 1745, Sir John, who remained in this place, was applied to, and in the open green close by the house he drilled the various trades before they went on active duty. About this period the Earl of Kilmarnock and Marquis of Tullibardine called upon him to ask his advice; he earnestly implored them not to enter upon that enterprise, which cost the one his life and made the other an exile for ever. It must appear obvious that during the unfortunate 1715 and 45, the men of Greenock were loyal to the House of Hanover, and however we may admire the exalted devotion of the prince's army,[2] and also deplore the fearful winding up of the tragedy where so many noble victims were

---

1. The Duke was a frequent visitor at Greenock house, and when His Grace intended to return an impress party were sent to man the barge. The individuals thus seized "came nothing loath" in consequence of the great kindness with which they were treated on these occasions, in not only receiving a silver Jacobus or two, but a supply of the good beverage on both sides of the Clyde.

2. The Chevalier's army never visited Greenock, in consequence of war vessels being moored at intervals from about the old Battery to above Port Glasgow. It is said that about 18 or 24 came to spy the land, and reached as far as Clune Brae, but on receiving the fire from the ships of war returned immediately to the headquarters at Glasgow.

sacrificed, yet there can be but one opinion as to the issue of a contest which secured to Britain its civil and religious liberty, and which raised this nation to its present greatness. In the neighbourhood of this house Sir John mustered the different trades to walk the fair for the protection of property, which was often carried off by Rob Roy and his men as well as other marauders, and though this exhibition latterly became a mere pageant, it was not abolished till 1822.

The following Act of Parliament, granted in 1696 by King William, with the consent and advice of the Estates in Parliament, to Sir John, will show its importance:— "Grants to Sir John Shaw, his airs and successors for ever, the right and priviledges of three fairs yearly to be held in the town of Greenock." And after specifying the days in which these fairs should be held, there is the following concluding clause:— "With the haill priviledges, profits, tolls, customs, and casualties of the said fairs and rnercats, with power to the said Sir John Shaw and his foresaids, by themselves and others in their names, to cause proclaim *and ryde the said fairs, and to make such orders and directions for the right government thereof as they see fit,* and to take, uplift, and dispose upon the said profits, tolls, customs and casualties of the same, with all confiscations and amerciaments arising by any thefts, ryots, bloods and battereis, that may happen to fall out thereat, and to do all other things competent in the like cases to be done, by any having the right and priviledges of keeping free fairs and mercats within this kingdom."

A very imperfect idea can now be formed of the beauty and extent of the baronial policy. Mr. Alexander Drummond, his Majesty's Consul at Tripoli, takes notice of this place, when speaking of Vabro in Italy:

"Here the Count de Merci possesses a beautiful house, that stands upon the top of the hill, with fine terraced gardens sloping down to the river side, which yield a delicious prospect to the eye; yet beautiful as this situation is, the house of Greenock would have been infinitely more noble, had it been, according to the original plan, above the terrace, with the street opening down to the harbour: indeed, in that case, it would have been the most lordly site in Europe."

From the house there was a fine row of trees, which led to a pleasant retreat at the top of the Whin Hill containing many apartments, and it is well known that this hill was entirely covered with wood till 1782. Where Regent Street, etc., now stands was also covered with wood till 1809, when this beautiful ornament to the town also disappeared. The peculiar advantages which the inhabitants of the policy enjoy, in being exempted from town taxes, has made this place, independent of its fine situation, much sought after. The name of this wood was popularly known as Lovie's Wood, and here many a happy school-boy hour was spent in the intervals between studying Horace or some teasing Mathematical problem; yet here, amidst all the noisy glee of as rich a scene as can well be remembered—to use Gray's beautiful lines—

> "Alas! regardless of their doom,
> The little urchins play;
> No dread have they of ills to come,
> No care beyond a day."

Within the limits of the policy, and on the terrace alluded to by Mr. Drummond, it is intended to erect a monument, at once useful and ornamental, to the memory of James Watt, our illustrious townsman. It is to be an elegant building, capable of containing the Greenock Library, instituted in 1783, and containing about 7000 volumes. In a hall, fitted up for the purpose, is to be placed a statue of Mr. Watt, executed in Chantry's happiest manner. The sum for the statue was raised by subscription, and amounts to £1700, and Mr. Watt of Soho intends to give the necessary sum for the erection of the building amounting to about £3000.

When the Library was first instituted it was kept in Mr. Wilson's school-room, Royal Closs,[1] who was first Librarian. It is at present in a commodious room above the Green Market. The Rev. John Dunn is at present librarian.

The new Coffee Room, at the corner of the Square, was commenced in 1820 and finished the same year. The reason of this new erection was in consequence of a difference having arisen between a number of the subscribers and the proprieters of the Exchange Buildings. As the secession was almost immediate, or at least before the new room was built, the members were accommodated with a room in the White Hart Inn, then unlet. The expense of this erection amounted to nearly £2500, and certainly there are few rooms more splendid, having a fine cupola, and otherwise finished in an elegant manner. This room, like the other, is well supplied with various papers, etc., and is equally liberal in allowing privileges to all strangers, without introduction, for six weeks.

In 1810 the Jail, or Bridewell, was built. It is situated behind the Mid Parish Church, in a fine open space, enclosed with a wall, and is built something in the style of an old castle, having two towers in front, with battlements at the top. This is the only place occupied as a prison for criminals, and contains a debtor's apartment, besides a place where the criminals labour. Previous to its erection the Jail, or Black Hole, was in front of the Town's House, but the first "durance vile" which was used in Greenock was a thatched house at the bottom of Broad Closs, where the

---

1. It is a fact not generally known that the two guns at the principal entrance belonged to one of the Spanish Armada, which was wrecked at Pencores Castle, and a number from the same vessel are placed about the quays.

Jugs[1] were hung *in terrorem* of offenders; and another set of Jugs were hung for the same laudable purpose at the Nest Quayage, in a house called the Inspector's Land. The Keep, or, as it was called, massy-more of the Mansion-house, was afterwards used as a prison, and continued to be so till after the year 1765, when the Town Buildings were erected.

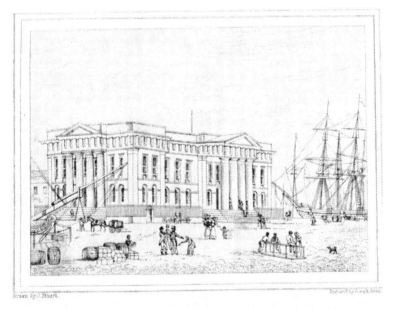

CUSTOM HOUSE.

Engraved for Weir's History of Greenock.

In 1818 an extensive building was erected on the East Quay for the customs and excise, but known as the Custom House. It is

---

1. Jug or jugs is slang for jail. In this context it seems to refer some object of dread like the stocks or shackles. Jugate can mean to couple or yoke as you would an ox.—GP

a great ornament to the town, and, from its situation, being on the centre of the quay where the steamboats arrive, is seen to much advantage by strangers either visiting or passing the port. It has a fine esplanade in front, from which there is a delightful view of the opposite coast. The structure is handsome, having an elegant portico, in the Grecian Doric order of architecture, supporting a pediment. It has also another front towards the south-east, which is the entrance to the excise department. The rooms are all elegantly fitted up, and the long room of the Custom House is about 76 feet by 42, and 26 high. The building cost altogether about £30,000. As immediately connected with this building we subjoin the following list, which gives some idea of the progressive rise of the trade of the Clyde in this particular department:

Account of the Gross Receipt of the Customs at the Port of Greenock, in the years 1728 till 1828.

£.	s.	d.	£.	s.	d.
1728, ... 15,231	4	4 1/2	1822,[1] ...263,464	8	10 1/2
1745, ... 15,831	3	9 1/2	1823,.....322,730	13	7 3/4
1770, ... 57,336	6	10 1/2	1824,.....318,806	19	1 1/2
1794, ... 77,680	6	0 3/4	1825,.....414,447	2	7
1798, ... 141,853	19	10	1826,.....395,774	5	5 1/4
1802, ... 211,087	2	8	1827,.....464,813	8	0 3/4
1814, ... 376,713	16	9 1/4	1828,.....455,596	13	3 1/2

Account of the number of Registered Vessels belonging to the Port of Greenock (exclusive of the Creeks of Rothesay, Ban, and Tobermorry), with their Tonnage and Men, for the years ending 31st December, 1825, till 1828.

---

1. The duties on Tobacco, Coffee, and Pepper were collected by the Excise from 5th July, 1819, till 5th April, 1825, when all the Import Duties of Excise were transferred to the Customs.

	No.	Tons.	Men.
1825, ...	241	29,054$\frac{89}{94}$	1987
1826, ...	235	21,634$\frac{78}{94}$	1861
1827, ...	238	30,940$\frac{25}{44}$	2090
1828, ...	249	31,929$\frac{75}{94}$	2210

Account of the Number and Tonnage of Vessels entered Inwards and cleared Outwards to Foreign Parts with Cargoes, in the year ended 5th January, 1784, till 1829.

| | INWARDS. | | | | OUTWARDS. | | | |
| | British. | | Foreign. | | British. | | Foreign. | |
	No.	Tons.	No.	Tons.	No.	Tons.	No.	Tons.
1784, ...	52	6569	4	530	63	7297	3	520
1789, ...	110	18678	12	1802	136	21489	10	1891
1794, ...	89	14807	17	3357	90	16953	13	2506
1799, ...	103	16760	19	4404	123	20516	19	4286
1804, ...	165	30802	25	5120	155	31896	20	5965
1809,[1] ..	88	20094	10	2095	127	25795	11	3030
1814, ...	163	40447	5	1007	186	43685	5	986
1819, ...	206	49774	26	6153	282	61168	29	6964
1823, ...	166	39345	22	5325	219	47414	25	6320
1825, ...	178	46156	18	4783	174	43216	17	5083
1826, ...	201	51249	21	6229	193	49079	18	6195
1827, ...	196	53898	8	2380	193	51430	7	2260
1828, ...	203	52266	11	4744	203	52896	11	3444
1829, ...	210	52721	13	3806	211	53757	10	3159

---

1. At this time the American Non-intercourse Decrees were in force, as well as those of Berlin and Milan.

Account of the Number and Tonnage of Vessels entered Inwards from and cleared Outwards to Ireland with Cargoes, in the year ended 5th January, 1784, till 1829.

	INWARDS.		OUTWARDS.	
	No.	Tons.	No.	Tons.
1784,	121	5225	134	5673
1789,	191	11649	120	7486
1794,	197	13926	165	11196
1799,	250	15250	221	13034
1804,	215	17624	168	12505
1809,	236	19807	173	14047
1814,	152	10870	117	9184
1819,	185	13649	165	11912
1823,	174	18201	170	17711
1829,	208	26325	250	32750

Opposite the Custom House is an elegant cast-iron Corinthian Pillar, cast by Caird & Co., Founders, and lighted by gas, to facilitate the approach of vessels by night to our harbours. A little distance from this, on the right, a Camera Obscura has been fitted up, and the profits arising from this exhibition are given to the Greenock Hospital.

The Renfrewshire Bank occupies a substantial house, built in 1811, on the line of Shaw Place. The time of its first establishment was in 1802, and it then occupied the low flat of the house in Hamilton Street, opposite Tanwork Closs. Like the Greenock Bank its business is very extensive, having various branch banks independent of its intercourse with all commercial districts.

Though possessing so large a population no gaswork was established here till 1828. The building is situated in the Glebe, and is a great ornament to the street. Notwithstanding of the strong prejudice[1] in having works of this kind in a populous neighbourhood from the offensive smell, no inconvenience has been felt on this score. It is but justice to an individual now in the dust to state that the first requisition calling the inhabitants together was in his hand-writing, and though others finished the work in a manner which must give satisfaction to everyone, both from the handsome structure and the purity of the gas produced, doing justice to that individual does not at all detract from their merits. The profits arising from the consumption of gas is to aid the town's funds, and the public are well aware that its necessities require every fair and legitimate means of doing so. From a statement published on the 26th June, 1829, it appears that the total cost of works, etc., is £8731 9s—revenue, £2054 11a 6d; which, after deducting outlays and interest, leaves a balance in favour of the town, £981 9s 2d.

The Flesh Market, which is situated in Market Street, was first built in 1764, and rebuilt in 1815. It contains 16 stalls, and has a most convenient slaughter-house behind. The first cow which was killed there was by James Bartlemore: it was paraded through the town dressed in ribbons, with the town-drum beating before it. The Fish Market is situated at the Mid Quay, is well fitted up, and convenient for this purpose.[2]

The Butter Market, or, as it is called, the Green Market, is immediately under the Library, at the east end of Market Street,

1. As an instance in point, an old lady called in the neighbourhood of the gaswork about four mouths before its completion, and having looked out of the window, then open, asked if this was the gaswork? On being told it was, she begged to have the window shut as the smell was truly horrible.
2. It is worth noticing that the guns planted at the extremities of this building, for protecting the corners from injury by carriages passing, belonged to the Adventure discovery ship when under the command of the celebrated circumnavigator, Captain Cook.

and is but partially used for this purpose. Greenock possesses no regular Meat Market, etc., but did so many years ago. The first situation was foot of Tanwork Closs, and afterwards at the head of Watson's Lane.

The Post Office has never possessed any building entirely for itself, and consequently the frequent movements from one place to another have been at the suggestion of the postmaster of the day. It has at last settled in the opening at the head of Cross-shore Street, named Watt Place. The revenue from this establishment in 1797 was £2800, and in 1828 the sum of £4183 was collected.

Independent of the public buildings belonging to the town, or those which have been raised by subscription, there are other places, the property of private individuals, which ought not to be omitted. The White Hart, a large and commodious inn situated near the Square, was built about 1770, but lately it was raised upon, and otherwise much improved; this house contains 9 sitting-rooms and 17 bed-rooms. The Gardeners' Hall is situated in Manse Lane, the Buck's Head Inn and Mason Lodge in Hamilton Street, and the George Inn at the East Breast.

About 1740 a Bridge was thrown across the stream which joins the sea near Mr. Scott's building yard, and was known by the name of Finnart Burn. This was the first erection of the kind in the neighbourhood. Latterly two other Bridges were built across the same water, and have all been improved and enlarged since their first erection. About fifty years ago there was no Bridge at the east of the town; the substitute for this was the old rudder of a vessel, which continued till the erection of Ling Burn Bridge (not Deling Burn), and in 1777 the Bridge near to Mr. Moscript's church was erected.

About seventy years ago the roads were wretched, and a Marshal Wade was much wanted to procure the blessing of a good pathway the unshod travellers. The road to Gourock, for instance, was by the shore-side, and if strong gales produced a high tide an embargo was laid upon all travellers till the weather moderated and the joint influences of Boreas and Neptune permitted a free passage. The dates are vague and uncertain as to the period when the various roads were commenced and finished, and we believe few are anxious to ascertain the point, seeing that the task has been accomplished in a manner which ensures comfort as well as pleasant and easy travelling.

WHITE HART INN &c?

Engraved for the History of Greenock

*　　*　　*　　*　　*

Chapter 6.
DEFENCES AND NAVAL INTEREST.

THE first battery that was raised for protecting the town was in 1763. It was of rude architecture, and got up hurriedly in consequence of various reports of armed vessels having been seen approaching the Clyde; it mounted twelve 24-pounders, and was situated near the Ropework Quay. On the breaking out of the war between Great Britain and the American colonies in 1776, Lord Frederick Campbell,[1] with the Western Fencibles, were ordered to Greenock, and in a short time made various additions to the fort. The loyalty of the town at this period was aroused to a very high degree; every man stood forward condemning the rebellion, and Mr. Thomas Moore, the accomplished poet, in his late travels proved, from facts which have never been contradicted, that self-interest on the part of many of the colonists and French jealousy were the means of wresting this growing state from the sceptre and authority of Great Britain. The fertile valleys of France soon felt the fearful retribution, for when La Fayette and his soldiers returned, the word Liberty was fresh upon their lips, and the tyranny of Louis and his nobles was quenched in an ocean of blood. Britain, under the guidance of Providence, has resisted every effort of her foes, and stood the fiery ordeal almost single-handed till her greatest enemy perished on the bleak island of St. Helena, while her shores had never been traced by the foot of a

---

1. The first public dinner ever given in Greenock, at the town's expense, was to Lord Frederick Campbell and his officers for their industry in putting the town in a state of defence, and for the conduct of the soldiers in their intercourse with the inhabitants.

foreign enemy. We have already said that, on the breaking out of the American war in 1776, the people of Greenock rallied faithfully around their Sovereign, and, in proof of this, the following placards were posted on the corners of our streets from the two great bodies which then composed the most important part of the population:

"Greenock, 23rd January, 1776."

"Sundry Merchants in Greenock, being desirous to promote the manning of His Majesty's Navy with able seamen, having raised by subscription a sum of money for that purpose, do hereby offer a Reward of One Guinea, over and above His Majesty's Bounty, to each of the first Sixty able Seamen belonging to the towns of Greenock, Crawfordsdyke, Gourock, and Inverkipp, not above Fifty nor under Eighteen years of age, who shall voluntarily enter to serve in His Majesty's Navy with Lieutenant Henry Constobadie, or the Commanding Officer in Greenock for the time, betwixt and the twenty-ninth of February next; to be paid by Joseph Tucker, Merchant in Greenock, upon a Certificate from the said Lieutenant Constobadie, or the Commanding Officer of the time."

"The Buss Herring Fishing Society of Greenock, impressed with a just abhorrence of the unnatural Rebellion in America, tending to the subversion of the present happy establishment, under the wisest and most moderate Government, do therefore offer One Guinea of Bounty, over and above His Majesty's royal Bounty, to the first Hundred able Seamen, who shall betwixt and the first day of March next enter under Lieutenant Henry Constobadie, of His Majesty's Navy, now at Greenock, from whom proper Certificates must be procured and lodged with Mr. James Taylor, Merchant in Greenock, who will order immediate payment of the Society's Bounty."

The town also gave a bounty, and in a short time a number of enterprising and excellent seamen were added to the Navy.

When the gallant and humane Frenchman, M. Thurot, entered the channel with his squadron, a universal alarm was given, not only to Greenock but to the surrounding country. And this received a great impulse from the fact of his having captured a vessel off the Craig of Ailsa. It was at this period that a temporary fort was erected containing twelve 24-pounders, and, in addition to this, brass field-pieces were stationed along the road leading to the fort and on the Ropework Quay. It was not, however, till after the breaking out of the revolutionary war that this place underwent a complete change, and Fort Jervis, with its magazines, etc., was completed in 1797. Prior to this, and in 1795, Roger Stewart, Esq., who took a deep interest in the town, wrote Lord Adam Gordon concerning the state of the battery, and to have it properly provided, and the following answer will show the manner in which these places of defence were kept up, as also the sentiments of government on this interesting subject:—

"Abbey, Edinburgh, 27th May, 1795."

"SIR,—When batteries were erected for the protection of the different towns on the coast of Scotland, a rule was established, that the guns, shot, and small stores should be furnished by the Ordnance; and the powder, and the expense of placing the platforms for the guns, should be defrayed by the inhabitants of the towns. As this rule is still to be adhered to, I am now to desire that you will report to me the quantity of shot and small store you now have for the use of your Battery, which I shall transmit to the Board of Ordnance, that whatever is wanting may be supplied by them. You will also be pleased to report to me the number and size of your guns; the quantity of gunpowder now in your possession; with the state and condition of the guns, carriages, platforms, and storehouses; that whatever articles are wanting may be provided, and repairs ordered where necessary, that your Battery may be put in a proper state of defence.

"I have the honour to be,

"SIR,

"Your most obedient humble Servant,
"A.D. GORDON, General.

"Chief Magistrate, Greenock."

When Thurot's little squadron was captured, which gave so much alarm to Greenock, the guns were fired as a signal for rejoicing, but during the hours of merriment a gun unfortunately burst, which killed two men, and a piece of the shattered ordnance, weighing about 24 pounds, flew over the Ropework and sunk in the Glebe, three feet deep. This fort continued till about 1808, bristling its loud-mouthed cannon towards the wave, but was dismantled in 1809, and in 1812 the fort, about two miles from the town, was erected. What gave rise to this erection was the audacity of some American cruizers[1] coming far up the channel, and the fact of a number of merchant vessels having been captured two days after leaving the port.

This fort was dismantled in 1820, in consequence of the disturbed state of the country, by an order received from Government to the Lord of the Manor. The guns now lying in Dumbarton Castle, with all their mounting, and the ammunition were also transported to the same place.

Few places during the war evinced more loyalty to Government than Greenock; Volunteers were raised, the Mass Regiment formed, and, in addition to this, the Artillery and Rifle Corps were established. A very large subscription was procured to aid the Government in prosecuting the war, and the following subscription to assist the country in establishing a military force

1. When M'K——r was tried for abstracting money from a certain letter, when he was in the Post Office, an individual, who could have been a material witness, took a trip to the land of liberty; he there met a number of young men, at a convivial party, who were loud in condemning this country and its institutions. The enraged man rose from his seat and told them they were unlike Scotchmen to rail at the land which gave them birth, "but, to be plain," added he, none of you dare return, except myself."

was entered into. As it may be curious, as a document, the names are given, with their amount.

"WE, Subscribers, hereby promise to pay to the Collector of the Land Tax of the County of Renfrew, the sums annexed to our respective Subscriptions, for the purpose of establishing a Military Force for the Internal Defence and Security of the County of Renfrew, as fixed by the Minutes of a Meeting of the Landed Proprietors, held at Renfrew, the Twentieth day of June, Seventeen Hundred and Ninety-four."

Roger Stewart, for the—
Town of Greenock £52 10 0
Roger Stewart, for self...... 10 10 0
Gabriel Lang 5 5 0
James Gemmell, ... 10 10 0
Hugh Crawford 5 5 0
John Dunlop 6 6 0
Walter Ritchie 5 5 0
Hugh Moody 5 5 0
Archibald Campbell 5 5 0
Robert Steuart 6 6 0
Andrew Anderson 5 5 0
William Fullarton 5 5 0
Alexander Dunlop 5 5 0
James Bell 5 5 0
James Leitch, senior 5 5 0
Duncan M'Naught 5 5 0
Gabriel Wood 5 5 0
Roger Stewart, for Hugh—
Crawfurd, Kilblain 5 5 0
Andrew Anderson, for—
Gavin Fullarton 4 4 0
Andrew Hill 2 2 0
George Robertson 5 5 0

Donald M'Lachlan £1 1 0
Alexander Wood 1 1 0
Colin Menzies 1 1 0
Burrow & Lawson 5 5 0
John Hamilton 5 5 0
Alan Kerr 2 2 0
James Wood 2 2 0
Thomas Ramsay 2 2 0
Alexander Crawford   2 2 0
Dug. Ferguson, for self—
and father 2 2 0
James & John Rankin 5 5 0
James Ewing, junior 1 1 0
Robert Lee, junior, for self—
and Robert Lee, senior, .. 5 5 0
William Graham 2 2 0
William Robertson 1 1 0
John M'Cunn 2 2 0
Archibald Stewart 2 2 0
William Scott 5 5 0
James Anderson 2 2 0
Alexander M'Arthur 2 2 0
Walter Buchanan 2 2 0
David Williamson 1 1 0

James Scott	5 5 0		Robert Bog	5 5 0
James Anderson	5 5 0		James Blair	2 2 0
John Wright	7 7 0		James Miller	5 5 0
James Bogle	5 5 0		Hugh Crawford, junior	1 1 0
John Forbes	1 1 0		John M'Kechnie	1 1 0
Thomas M'Cunn	5 5 0		A. & J. Robertson & Co.	5 5 0
John Scott	5 5 0		Archibald Baine	1 1 0
John Kippen	5 5 0		Francis Garden	5 5 0
Pollock Campbell	5 5 0		Robert Sinclair	2 2 0
Charles Ogilvie	5 5 0		James Fraser	1 1 0
John Esdale	1 1 0		Robert Baine	3 3 0
John Kerr	1 1 0		George Ker & Co.	1 1 0
Robert Caldwell	3 3 0		Brown & Co. of Saltcoats—	
John Holmes	1 1 0		Ropework	5 5 0
Duncan Campbell	1 1 0		Neil Campbell	5 5 0
Ninian Spence	5 5 0		Lewis Gellie	5 5 0
Robert Lindsay	1 1 0		James Noble	1 1 0
James Park	1 1 0		Robert M'Conechy	1 1 0
Archibald Fleeming	5 5 0		John and Wm. Brownlie	2 2 9
Graham M'Farlane	1 1 0		Alexander Dunlop, for—	
James Malcolm	5 5 0		James Knox	5 5 0
Duncan M'Kellar	1 1 0		Campbell, Lee & Co.	5 5 0
C. Campbell	1 1 0		Nathan Wilson	1 1 0
Alexander Tait	1 1 0		John and Wm. Adam,	1 1 0
James Hunter	1 1 0		J. M'Donald	1 1 0
Robert M'Fie	1 1 0		Thomas Crawford	1 1 0
John Johnston	1 1 0		John Weir	1 1 0
Alexander M'Kinlay	1 1 0		Charles Wallace	1 1 0
Peter Warnock	2 12 6		Total	£378 10 0

On receiving this subscription, Mr. M'Dowall, M.P., wrote as follows:—"The town of Greenock has been held out as remarkable for assisting the country, with much liberality, independent of their own Volunteers."

The raising of the men, when "Mother Casey"[1] paraded the street in a boat seemingly rowed by many who are still alive, showed the active spirit which prevailed, and when the alarm was given, in consequence of a Dutch frigate, which Captain Crawford steered into the Clyde, having reached the Tail of the Bank, every man was ready to "seek the bubble reputation in the cannon's mouth." But the most conspicuous instance was in the well-known *"Battle of Armady,"* when an alarm had been given that some French frigates were coming up to burn the town and the whole of our forces, consisting of the Volunteers, etc., were shipped on board a frigate, and the private ships, Neptune, St. Andrew, and Mercury. The willingness to encounter the enemy on this occasion was beyond all praise, and Government felt and acknowledged their alacrity. The public rejoicings, when any great battle was fought, were also a proof of how deeply the inhabitants felt for the glory of our country. The illumination for the battle of Trafalgar, which closed the glorious and eventful life of the gallant Nelson, was as universal as the event called for. It is a fact, not generally known, that it was in the arms of a Greenock seaman (a seaman who had been in almost all his victories) that this hero was conveyed to the cockpit after receiving his death-wound on the quarterdeck of the Victory. This noble fellow presented himself to an audience at the Theatre, a few months after the battle, and stated the fact to the audience as an apology for his calling the orchestra to play up "Rule Britannia." A similar scene occurred at Covent Garden Theatre about the same time, only with a greater variety of interesting incidents.

The loyalty of Greenock was never questioned till the unfortunate 8th of April, 1820, and, then, through misrepresentations, the "fair name" which existed for a century was attempted to be

---

1. Five hundred men were raised by this means, and were known by
    the name of the "Clyde Marine Volunteers."

sullied. In Blackwood's Magazine, Vol. VII., p. 91, are the following remarks:— "In at least three places, the King's standard is
assaulted by rebels, prepared for a regular campaign. We write on
19th April, 1820, and allude to Bonnymuir, Greenock, and
Huddersfield." To say the least, this is a false and most gratuitous
assertion. An event occurred here at that period, which had a most
unfortunate result; but how did it occur? On the day in question
the Port Glasgow Volunteers, who had been doing duty in Paisley
during the reign of Radicalism, were returning to their homes,
and were entrusted with three poor fellows, who were placed in a
cart, to escort to Greenock Jail. This was known from an early
period of the day, and crowds of tradesmen assembled in the
street. About two o'clock the party entered the town, and, in place
of shewing sympathy to the individuals concerned, they came
with drum and fife playing martial tunes. This certainly excited
the indignation of the crowd, and it is to be lamented that stones
were thrown at the military. This increased, and more particularly
on their leaving town, when, without reading the Riot Act,
without the orders of any Magistrate, and also against the orders
of Mr. C——ll, their commanding officer, they fired into the
midst of the crowd at different periods, till many lives were lost
and a number of individuals severely wounded. On this occasion
a miller, always esteemed a quiet individual, with a boy of about
12 years of age, behaved with bravery. They followed the soldiers
to the Bottle Work, and when they observed any musket levelled,
always attacked the individuals to injure their aim or otherwise
intimidate them. Though frequently fired at they escaped unhurt,
and returned to the town together recounting their exploits. The
miller was obliged to escape in consequence to America.[1]

---

1. On the same evening the excited feelings of the crowd prompted
   them to break open the jail and liberate the prisoners.

Some have attempted to question the loyalty of the town from the resistance made to the Impress Service, and it is well known that various mobs have arisen against those employed in this unpleasant duty. The earliest on record is known by the name of "Gentles' Mob," when Lieutenant Gentles was attacked, and took refuge in the Guard-house, foot of Cowgate; and the boat in which he came on shore was dragged up to the same place, and broken to pieces. Other serious riots occurred, but no lives were lost. To call in question the feelings of a community on this score amounts to nonsense. The Impress Service is one of cruelty, and cannot fail to excite the feelings in an extraordinary degree. Are men to be dragged away from the bosom of their families and from their homes without exciting the sympathy of those around them? Is a system of kidnapping, which we have condemned and abolished on the shores of Africa, to be practised in Britain, the land of boasted liberty? It is the legislature who can answer the question, and among the last acts of the benevolent Quinton Leitch was a series of resolutions recommending the legislature to adopt other measures, and which were read, along with other remarks, at a Meeting in the Town Hall, three years ago, on this important subject.

The rendezvous was kept at the Tar Pots for a short period, and was usually at the West Quay, from the window of which the British Union was always hung out.

Although the men of Greenock were always at their post at the hour of alarm, yet their courage was often wrought up unnecessarily to the "sticking point," through the waggery of a few who had indulged in the second bowl after dinner. The "man with the horn" on horseback, blowing through the town and depositing his large packets at the Post Office, was an instance of this kind. Similar was the mistake of a Jamaica fleet for a French squadron, and which was contradicted by Mr. Scott giving the true state of the case. Anecdotes of this kind might be multiplied, but as many of them relate to individuals still alive, or to those whose relations are amongst us, we avoid mentioning them lest the motive might be misunderstood and pain given, where every care has been taken to avoid this, either on private or public grounds. It is much better to be accused of withholding a little information, when the giving of it is of no great importance, and might only revive, in the breasts of some, feelings and emotions which are viewed differently in the hey-day of youth from what they are in old age.

*　　*　　*　　*　　*

Chapter 7.
RISE & SOCIAL PROGRESS.

HAVING noticed our principal public buildings, it may be proper to enter at some length into the rapid rise of a town, which has become, in so short a period, to be possessed of so many. From the smallest beginnings the mightiest cities on earth have entirely sprung: a time was when the surface of the globe contained but one dwelling; when Babylon, with its extensive walls, and Imperial Rome, with its palaces, showed no vestige of their future greatness. Greenock, about 200 years ago, had no symptoms of ever having possessed anything more than the straggling hut on the margin of the Clyde, or a few fishing boats on the bosom of its sunny bay. It never was the seat of any royal residence; it has had no parliamentary influence in sending a member to parliament; and though Pennant says, "that Sommerled, Thane of Argyle, raised a banditti in Ireland, which was landed at the Bay of St. Lawrence, to oppose Canmore, King of Scotland," we are not aware that here any mighty conflict ever occurred.

In 1636, we have already said, the first feu was ever granted, and it must have "progressed very slowly" (as Jonathan says), for in the year 1706 Greenock and Crawfordsdyke did not contain 1000 inhabitants. Crawfordsdyke, at this period, was of more importance—it contained a pier, which this town could not boast of: from this village part of the unfortunate expedition to the Isthmus of Darien in 1697 was fitted up. In connection with Cartsdyke, we may also state:— A little above the house of Cartsburn stood a cottage that gave birth to the celebrated donor of the equestrian statue of King William to the City of Glasgow, James M'Rae, who was long herd to the tenant of Hill-end, the great

great grandfather of the late H. Crawford. Tradition says that M'Rae offered to place the statue in Cartsdyke, but the then laird of Cartsburn (a very godly man) rejected it, wishing, in preference, that the influence of Mr. M'Rae might be exercised to have Cartsdyke made a parish. This Mr. M'Rae became the ancestor of the families of Glencairn, Orangefield, Houston, and Don. He lies interred in the churchyard of Monkton.

Some idea may be formed of how cheaply the African Company, etc., held our town, for they do not even mention it in the following correspondence:

"AT the Court of Directors of the Company of Scotland trading to Africa and the Indies, holden at Edinburgh, the 12th day of March, 1697, upon a Motion then made for directions how to conclude with the several Proprietors concerned in the Bay of Ardmore, for the Company's intended Salt Works,

Resolved, That Mr. William Dunlop, with the advice and assistance of Sir John Shaw, or any other of the Directors at Glasgow, be hereby empowered to conclude with the Heritors and Proprietors of the said Bay of Ardmore, and to take either a Feu or Tack of the next adjacent Lands and Yaire, equal to a perpetual right, at the present yearly rent. And if the present Mr. William Dunlop cannot agree on reasonable terms with the said Proprietors, to agree with Sir John Shaw for his Bay, etc. Ordered, That the said Mr. William Dunlop do, at the same time, with advice aforesaid, agree with such Proprietors of Coals in those pacts, as will give the most reasonable conditions to the Company for such quantities thereof as the Company shall have occasion for."

[Extracted by Order of the said Court.]

"Edinburgh, 25th March, 1697.

"REVEREND Sir,—The Directors are now of the belief, that it is the Company's interest to have in their hands all the Lands which the Heritors can pretend to be any manner of way damnified by the Company's Works; since probably they can always have it tenanted to better advantage than the present yearly rent. Sir John Shaw would have you bring everything to a readiness for signing upon the 9th or 10th day of next month, at which time he resolves positively to meet you at Glasgow, and questions not but he would help to bring all those gentlemen to reasonable terms.

I am, Reverend Sir,

Your most humble Servant."

"Edinburgh, 25th *March,* 1697.

"REVEREND Sir,—You may remember that the naming of Sir John Shaw's Bay in the Order of Court was put in by Sir John Shaw's own direction, for a blind to the rest, in order to get the better bargain. I could wish I was to act your part in this matter; for Mr. Cragg told me, and some few others, that Sir John's Bay was a very little thing, and excellent ground, fit for the work, and wished the Company would fall upon a way to hedge it from him handsomely. He was once resolved to have spoke of it to Sir John openly before the Directors; but, upon second thoughts, considered Sir John as a man that loved his interest, and, being master of money, would not part readily with a thing on easy terms, if once he was possessed of an opinion of its goodness. So that, were I in your place, he should get leave to be in jest, but I would be in earnest for the Company; and when I had completed his jest, would laugh at him, and tell him I had bitten the biter. This I communicated to Sir Francis Scott, Sir Patrick Scott, Newton Drummond, and Mr. Robert Blackwood only, who were mightily pleased with the thoughts of it, the three former of whom went out of town this week. So this I thought fit to let you know, to the end you may act as you please.

"I am, Reverend Sir,

"Your most faithful humble Servant."

Greenock, about this period, consisted of a row of houses, which commenced about East Quay Lane and terminated at Rue-end (a corruption of Row-end). A wide space intervened, and another row of houses commenced about Bell-entry, with their gables towards the shore, and terminated near the Old or West

Church. A specimen of the appearance of these houses may still be seen, nearly opposite to Mr. Clarke's Land, West Quay-head, which bears date above the doorway, 1667. Independent of these a range of houses stretched up the Vennel, and little groups occupied the space between the head and foot of Taylor's Closs and Burn Street westward, and a number of thatched houses were scattered about various parts of the town. The first slated house that ever was built in Greenock was about 1712, and was the property of a Bailie Butcher. It was situated at the corner of the lane leading from the foot of Highland Closs to the East Harbour. In 1716 there were only four houses covered with slate, one of which has been already noticed as at the corner of Cross-shore Street. About eighty years ago it was occupied by one M'Grigor, and was the principal, perhaps the only, inn in town. The sun-dial, for ascertaining the hour of the day, yet retains its place in the western corner, and the windows, despite of schoolboys and careless maids, are surprisingly entire, and still form a faithful, though brittle record, of the love effusions of its wayfaring inhabitants. Who can doubt that *la plus belle en Bordeaux est Mademoiselle Belfont,* or that Miss S——y S——h, or Miss N——y B——d of Irvine, and several others, whose names are there inscribed with the keen point of the diamond, were thought by their respective admirers the fairest of created beings? Their great grand-daughters, the toasts of the present day, will not take offence at the publication of these fondly cherished recollections, nor fastidiously dispute the line of propinquity which may recognise them as the representatives of the reigning beauties of 1749.

Opposite to the inn, and near the foot of the Broad Closs, stood the Prison—an ill-looking thatched house of one storey, and consequently of one apartment This was one of the places in which Jugs were displayed. In a word, the space described was the nucleus of the town of Greenock, Shaw Street being then the *High Street* of the town.

In the space betwixt the foot of Cross-shore Street and the foot of Broad Closs was the ancient Market Cross of Greenock. The usual places of resort for coal vessels, and other small craft bringing supplies to the town, was in the space occupied by the Tar Pots; hence the present Cross-shore Street—so named on account of its proximity at once to the shore and the cross. The cross was formed in the pavement, most probably by delineating the cardinal points of the compass within a circle, as appears in the Square; at all events, it bore the figures 1669 formed of white pebbles.

About 1755 the population reached 3500, and from this period increased rapidly. In consequence of this, buildings made their appearance in all directions, but more particularly in the new street which was opened from Rue-end to the Square. The first house built in this street was on the site of Mr. Brownlie's new land, and the first built in Hamilton Street was at the foot of Watson's Lane and corner of the Vennel. At the period of opening these streets, and long after, they had no names. The first land in the latter was built by a tailor, and the second by a smith. Like Tam O'Shanter and Souter Johnny they were like "very brithers,"

"And had been fou for days thegither."

In their cups the name of the street was often brought above board; the tailor insisted it should be called Needle Street, and the smith Hammer Street. Things remained thus in statua quo till the 8th August, 1775, when the Magistrates and Council having met, various representations were made regarding the streets having no names: Dalrymple Street being then known as the High Street; the Vennel as the Vennel; Cross-shore Street as Cross-shore Street; East Quay Lane as the lane leading to Sir John's Barge; and all the others, New Street, Nos. 1, 2, and 3. It was therefore ordered that the Laigh Street from Row-end be called "Dalrymple Street"; from Row-end to Square, "Cathcart Street";

from Square westward, "Hamilton Street"; Square to Mid Quay, "William Street"; from Poultry Market, etc., westward, "Mercate Street"; and from Laigh Street to Vennel, "Charles Street." At this period no other places had names. To trace the opening of streets in other directions would be absolutely superfluous, as this is in the remembrance of almost all. Where the town stands was formerly gardens, or covered with wood, and in the neighbourhood of what is known as "Lover's Lane," but a few years ago, some beautiful trees stood. Near to the Slaughter-house, and all along Tobago Street, were trees and rich gardens. In the garden about the foot of Ann Street a singular anecdote is told of the nightingale, a bird which has almost never been known to come farther north than Lancashire; yet it would appear to have been, for a time, a nocturnal visitant in this quarter. The authenticity of the following communication on the subject can be depended upon:—

"Betwixt forty and fifty years ago, and for many subsequent ones, the space of ground bounded on the Cowgate by the east, the Vennel on the north, the foot of and approach to Ann Street, etc., on the south and west, and which now forms the east-end of Tobago Street, the whole of Buccleugh Street, and is, besides, the site of several stately tenements of land, wrights' shops, etc., was a large and elegant garden, belonging to and possessed by the deceased Mr. James Scott, some of whose descendants, I believe, still reside in Greenock."——"My parents," continues the writer, "who are now also deceased, occupied a house in the immediate vicinity of Mr. Scott's garden, and I have been assured, a thousand times I dare say, by them both, that a nightingale, at least a bird that sung by night, visited the garden about the period above-mentioned for two consecutive summers to the great entertainment of the neighbours, and indeed of the major part of our worthy town's folk, who used to assemble in crowds about ten o'clock at night, and continue delightedly listening to the warbling stranger until the rising of the sun, which had invariably the effect of rendering him mute."

The fact, as now stated, is highly interesting, as regards the natural history of this singular bird. We have no feathered warbler that sings by night, except itself, although it is perfectly certain that, in the neighbourhood of the Carron Works, music has been heard from the adjoining grove, the birds mistaking the blaze of light for that of the rising sun.

After what has been mentioned of the almost talismanic appearance of this populous town, it must convince everyone that, however rich it may be in its resources, however extensive in its manufactures, that it is indeed but a few years since any importance could be attached to it. Washington Irving has given a most ingenious account of Rip Van Winkle's sleep among the Kaatskill mountains for a period of twenty years, and by this means has brought to view the changes of a most important period of American history. Let us, therefore, suppose some honest Greenockian to have indulged in a similar nap, and, on retracing his various scenes of infancy, etc., would he not, like Rip, be apt to say, "This is not me—this is not my town," but, pointing significantly to Gourock or Port-Glasgow, "that's it yonder?

"The principal streets are those already mentioned, and though the town has rather an irregular appearance, it contains many excellent buildings. It is evidently stretching towards the west, and many places, which were considered quite retired and in the country, form part of the streets. Those streets which have been planned lately are spacious, and forming rapidly. A number of beautiful villas are scattered from east to west, and give the stranger a highly favourable idea of the wealth as well as the taste of the inhabitants. The population in 1791 had arisen to 15,000, in 1801 it had increased to 18,400, in 1811 to 20,580, in 1821 to 23,500, and in the present year it amounts to about 27,000, including seamen, which must always be considered as forming an efficient part of the population of any seaport town. The increase of population is the most accurate means of ascertaining the extension or improvement of a town, and, judging by this, Greenock cannot be said to be falling off. One branch of its commerce may be depressed, or another may be influenced by changes or circumstances, but when a gradual rise takes place in the number of its inhabitants something must be the cause, and that must be, more or less, a degree of prosperity.

* * * * *

Chapter 8.
THE HARBOURS, TRADE & NAVIGATION.

WE now turn to the Quays—that one thing, above all others, which has made Greenock the important spot it is; and it is from this alone that she can date, not only her origin, but also her gradual improvement. The bay of Greenock is called in the document, at page 72, "Sir John's Little Bay," and at the time this was penned, namely, in 1697, the site of our spacious harbours was a fine sandy shore, washed by the waves. In 1696 and 1700 Sir John made application to the Scottish Parliament for public aid to build a harbour at Greenock, but both his applications were unsuccessful. Though thus frustrated the measure was of too much importance to be overlooked. At this time the only pier, or landing place, was at Sir John's Quay, where his barge was stationed, and was of less importance than the pier at Gourock. Vessels arriving discharged their cargoes at Cartsdyke breast, or were run upon the shore near Cross-shore Street. The inhabitants, however, saw the advantages which would result from having a commodious harbour, and they made a contract with the Superior by which they agreed that an assessment of 1s. 4d. Sterling should be raised from every sack of malt brewed into ale within the limits of the town, the money so levied to be applied in liqui-dating the expense of building a proper pier and forming the harbour. The work was begun at the period of the Union in 1707, and a capacious harbour laid out, containing upwards of ten Scotch acres, by building a kind of circular pier, with a tongue, or what is called the Mid Quay, in the centre. Some idea may be formed of the place by looking at the Port-Glasgow harbours, which   were   built   afterwards   on   the   exact model. These were formidable works and the greatest of the kind in Scotland, and incurred an expense of more than 100,000 merks Scots, which was equal to £5555 11s 1d. These works were completed about 1710, and on the 16th September of same year, Greenock was established a Custom House port and a branch of Port-Glasgow. The debt contracted alarmed the inhabitants very much, but such were the facilities to trade created by this new erection, that in 1740 the population was more than trebled and the sums advanced were paid up, leaving a clear surplus of 27,000 merks Scots or £1500 sterling. In 1783 the whole harbour dues amounted to £111 4s. 8d.; in 1792 £812 9s. was collected. Of late years the harbours may be said to have been entirely rebuilt, no vestiges of the old being seen all around, and certainly their present complete state reflects great credit on those who superintended and executed these splendid works. The first Act of Parliament for regulating the affairs of the harbours was obtained in 1773; another Act was obtained in 1789; a third Act in 1801; a fourth in 1803; a fifth in 1810; and a sixth Act in 1817.

The Harbours and New Dry Dock, including, as appertaining to the same estate, the lot of ground for warehouses at West Quay—the lot where the Dock Engine and Mr. Fish's Sail-loft stands—all the lots on the easternmost breast, used as Bonding Yards for mahogany, etc., with all the Sheds on different Quays, have cost £119,000. This, it may be remarked, includes the sum of £10,064 6s. 5d., paid in manner following by the Trustees of the Harbour to the Managers of the Town Proper.—In November, 1806, for value of Sheds, as per report of Messrs. John Laird, Duncan M'Naught, and Thomas Ramsay, £2286 14s. 5d. In March, 1807, for feu right to Shore Property, opposite to Mr. George Kerr and Mr. Gammell's property at West Breast, etc., £4902 6s. 2d. Some misunderstanding occurred at this time as to the exact proportion of annual Feu Duty for which the Harbour Trust became liable, and it was not until August, 1811, that the matter was finally arranged.—At that time a calculation of all the Feu Duties paid by the Town on account of the Harbour from 1773 was made up, which, including interest, amounted to £2875 5s. 10d., which sum was then paid by the Harbour Trustees to the Town Managers. At the same time the sum of £37 13s. 2d., and double that sum every nineteenth year, was fixed upon as the proportion of annual Feu Duty payable by the Trustees of the Harbour in relief of the Town, and this, of course, has been regularly accounted for ever since. After paying the Town for its Harbour right, the Trustees went along eastward, buying up the seaward rights of M'Gilp's heirs, Thomas Ewing's heirs, M'Gown's heirs, and of all others eastward to Delingburn—all of which have been settled.

The Town Proper reserved the exclusive right to the Anchorages, Dues on Coals, etc., coming to the Harbours. The Revenue arising from this source is not pledged for any part of the Debt of the Harbour, and it is plain that the extension of the Port has caused a great increase of the Anchorages, etc., and thereby given very efficient aid to the Revenue of the Town.

The works at the Harbour being finished, the Superior being paid grassum of the new Harbour, the Town and all Feuars having their shoreward rights bought up at an outlay short of £120,000, the sum authorised by Parliament to be borrowed for extending the Harbours and constructing the Dock—the question follows, what is the Estate worth? The Revenue of the Harbours, including Shed Dues, Dock Dues, Rents of Lofts, Enclosures, etc., appertaining to the Trust, is upwards of Nine Thousand Pounds per annum, with every appearance of increase.

In 1750 the following letter was addressed by Sir John Schaw (the liberal and enlightened gentleman who granted the charter in 1751), on the subject of the Harbours. Anything which could come from his pen should be treasured up, as he was to Greenock its greatest benefactor:—

"Greenock House, 8th *October,* 1750.

"Sir John Schaw, having considered the contents of the memorial from the Feuars and Sub-Feuars of the Town of Greenock, approves extremely of the scheme they propose of building a Breast of communication along the three Quays, with a row of Cellars on the land side, and will give his consent to Lord Cathcart's subfeuing to them the ground to the North of the inside Quay, which they design to begin that work upon. As he continues to have the good of the Town at heart as much as he ever had, he is willing either to let them have a nineteen years' tack of the Anchorage of the Harbour, at a rate which he thinks will be of assistance to the present funds of the Town, or to give them so much out of the yearly Anchorage, and to give them permission to build Cranes and Weigh-houses in such places as shall be judged necessary, with a full right to the Dues that will arise from them, which he expects, with the present funds, will be more than sufficient for the present and future cleansing of the Harbours and Quays, to which it ought to be immediately applied. He recommends to the Town to build the intended Breast and Cellars (after the same manner as they propose to build the Church), and as the Cellars in the Royal Closs yield ten per cent. interest for the money expended in building them, it is hoped it will not be difficult to find the sum necessary for that purpose, which in the course of years coming to be paid off, there will continue to arise a constant increase to the Town's Revenue.

"Sir John recommends to the Feuars, with the greatest earnestness, to consider with attention all possible means of increasing their funds, and of finding out others, that public works may be kept up with solidity when executed, and undertaken with expedition when found necessary, for the future; which they will find the most valuable advice can be given them.

"Sir John expects that the Feuars will immediately renew the assessment on malt, for fifteen years after the expiration of the present contract, and that they will strengthen it with all the additions they possibly can.

(Signed)   "JOHN SCHAW."

In connection with the Quays, a Dry Dock was built by a joint stock company in 1785, and cost £4000. In consequence of the trade of the port extending, and the old dock being found inconvenient to admit vessels of a large size, the following petition was presented to the Harbour Trustees:—

"To the Honourable the Magistrates and Town Council of Greenock.
"The Humble Petition of the Subscribers,
Merchants in Greenock.

"SHEWETH,

"That it is not necessary to use many words to convince any person concerned, or at all observant of the trade of this growing seaport, that two Graving Docks, and one of them altogether private property, are quite inadequate for the despatch of business. A Vessel may, and frequently does lie by the walls for weeks together, waiting the turn of admission, and it is obvious in this way, it must happen, that great inconvenience and positive loss is sustained by the Owners, and their projected voyages and plans frustrated and deranged irretrievably.

"That to remedy this, the Trade beseech your Honours to give immediate directions for the formation of a new Dry Dock, in such part of the Harbours as may be judged most convenient; and little doubt can be entertained that the necessary expense of it would be very soon got subscribed in shares, in the same way as was done in the case of the Old Dock.

(Signed)

"Thos. Alexander & Co.	Dun. M'Naught & Co.
M'Gowns, Watson, & Co.	William Galbraith & Co.
David Hyde & Co.	Ewing, Miller, & Co.
Shannan, Stewart, & Co.	Q. & J. Leitch.
Roger Stewart & Sons.	James Oughterson.
Robert Ewing & Co.	Gregor M'Gregor.
Robert Campbell & Co,	John Hamilton & Co.
Thos. Ramsay & Co.	Wilson & M'Lellan.
John Holmes & Co.	James Robertson.
Alan Ker & Co.	James Duncan.

Stevenson, Miller, & Co.   Lang, Baine, & Co.
Stuart & Rennie."

In reply the Petitioners were informed that the Trustees had no power to build a Dock on the principle proposed in the petition, but having authority to construct a Dock connected with the Harbour Trust their attention would be given to the measure. Accordingly, soon thereafter, at a Meeting of Trustees, Mr. Rennie's plans for Docks in the New East Harbour were examined. By Mr. Rennie two Docks were proposed alongside of each other—the large one on the site of the present Dock, and the smaller one in shore of it. At the gates of the largest it was intended to have sixteen feet of water at spring tides. Its estimated cost was £36,000. The expense of this Dock was considered by the Meeting as by far too heavy and the depth of water unnecessarily great, and as, in constructing a building of this kind, the gates and works at the entrance are a serious part of the expense, it was suggested that, in place of two Docks, one containing as much length as the two together would be more advisable. This being approved of, the then Master of Work, Mr. Burnet, was directed to make out a plan of a Dock (taking Mr. Rennie's plan for his guidance as to the inverted arch, mode of hanging gates, etc.) to be 36 feet wide at the gates, to have 18 inches more water than at the Old Dock, and to be excavated inside of the inverted arch, so as to obtain two feet more height betwixt the floor of the Dock and the top of the blocks—afterwards altered to 2 feet at the gates and $1\frac{1}{2}$ feet of excavation, thus making in all $3\frac{1}{2}$ feet greater depth than the Old Dock.

In conformity to these instructions the plan was executed, and sometime thereafter was laid before a Meeting of the Commissioners of the Harbours, when it had their unanimous approval. A written consent in terms of the Act of Parliament was endorsed on it, and subscribed by the Meeting, being thirteen in number, with a request on the part of the Commissioners, that the Trustees would get the building carried into effect as soon as the state of the funds would admit.

Nothing farther was done until the autumn of 1818, when the masonry of the Custom House, an edifice of great public utility, and acknowledged ornament to the port, was finished. The builder thereof, Mr. Donald Mathieson, having given the utmost satisfaction to the highly respectable architect[1] who planned and superintended the progress of that work, and his upright conduct wherever he had been employed being well known, the Trustees were induced to apply to him to undertake the building of the Dock, in strict conformity to the plans and specifications provided by Mr. Gibb.

Mr. Mathieson died shortly after commencing operations, and in 1824 the whole was finished, under the direction of Mr. William Aitken, at an expense of about £20,000. This is acknowledged to he a complete and elegant structure, while the ease and facility which it gives to examining and repairing vessels have brought many to the port. The Harbours, Docks, etc., as now completed, are allowed to be as commodious as any in the kingdom, and when the intended erection eastward is finished they will be scarcely surpassed anywhere. Mr. Hamilton, Master of Works, has communicated the following measurements, which will at once show the extent of the Quays and their accommodation:—

	Feet.
East Quay,	531
Entrance to Harbour,	105
Custom House Quay,	1035
Entrance to Harbour,	105
West Quay,	425

1. William Burn.—GP

```
Extreme length, from
East to West, .................................... 2201
Breadth of Piers, ............................ 60
```

At the head of the East India Quay, a fine arch, with gates, has been erected: the deputation of Commissioners of Customs and Excise, who visited the port in 1815, stipulated that this should be done. The cost of this erection was paid entirely out of the Harbour Police Fund.

The management of the Harbours is vested in its Commissioners (along with the Town Council), who are elected annually, and every ship-owner paying £12 per annum of harbour dues is eligible to be elected, while the paying £3 per annum qualifies for giving a vote.

Opposite the Quays is an extensive sand bank, which stretches from Dumbarton to a little below the town. The channel, by this means, is much narrowed, and the place where vessels generally cast anchor to remain for dispatches, etc., is about a mile and a half down, and known as the Tail of the Bank. Here there is a sufficient supply of water for vessels of the largest class, while the space is capable of containing an immense fleet, and the anchorage is excellent. The navigation of the Clyde is altogether very easy, consequently strangers have no difficulty in making out their course without the aid of a pilot. It is this which has often alarmed the inhabitants, lest the enemy might come up and attack the town, but the wind is its greatest protection, for the same breeze which would lead a vessel triumphantly up would keep her there, till she would probably be captured by the channel fleet, or till war-vessels arrived from Cork. In this way the Jason, Dutch frigate, was taken possession of at the Tail of the Bank, although, from the mutinous state of the crew, no injury was offered to the town or shipping.

The trade of Greenock consists of what is called Foreign and Coasting. Indeed, it may be said that there is no place where British enterprise has opened a market but Clyde vessels are to be found. The earliest vessel which crossed the Atlantic from Greenock was is July, 1684, and contained 22 persons, who were sentenced at Glasgow to be transported to Carolina for their share in resisting the oppression of these cruel times. The captain's name was James Gibson, who was represented as being very cruel to the poor prisoners, while his officers and crew used them in a still harsher manner. In 1685 part of the forces of Archibald, Earl of Argyle, who had come over from Holland, landed at Greenock. Of this occurrence, Wodrow gives the following interesting relation:

"Upon the first of May the Earl and his friends left Holland with a very few ships and a considerable number of arms. The money expended on these was mostly raised on the Earl's credit. The Duke of Monmouth, with the English gentlemen, had faithfully engaged not to stay above ten days after them in Holland; but it was a month before they landed in England. Whether this was done by design or necessarily, I do not determine. It was rumoured that this delay was advised, that the English forces might be poured down upon Scotland, and their game thus be easier in England. However, it is certain, the Duke of Monmouth was extremely concerned when the Earl's party was broke, and the Earl himself taken; and indeed his interest could not have met with a sorer dash. It is plain the English not keeping to the terms of agreement tended much to heighten the Earl's malheurs, and to the ruin of both.

"The Earl's intention was to have landed at Inveraray. In this, however, he was stiffly opposed by some of the gentlemen. A council of war was called, and there, contrary to the Earl's sentiments, it was resolved to make an invasion upon the Lowlands. The Earl calmly submitted, but indeed this step was mightily to their loss. The forces were accordingly transported the best way they could to Cowal in Argyllshire, and Sir John Cochrane, Colonel Elphinstoun, and Major Fullartoun were sent to the Lowlands.

"By this time the coasts were guarded, and some English frigates come up, so that Sir John durst not land in the Largs, as was projected, but put in towards Greenock.

"When they came within musket shot of the land, there appeared a body of horse upon the shore. Sir John having the command, ordered Colonel Elphinstoun to essay landing with about twenty men, which was all they could land at once for want of boats; but the thing being impracticable at that place, and the Colonel's orders being only to obey, in as far as reasonable, taking this to be the losing of so many men, he flatly refused.

"Sir John prevailed upon Major Fullartoun, with about a dozen of men, to attempt to land in another place near by, which he did under the fire of the Militia, and got safe ashore and into a sort of ditch for shelter. The printed account bears, 'That the Militia, seeing them ashore, gave over firing, and the young laird of Houston and Crawfordsburn came up to the Major, and another with him, and had some conversation, and passed their mutual words of honour to use no hostilities till the parley was over. After they had asked some questions at the Major, to his great surprise they discharged their pistols at him, which happily missed him, and he returned his, and killed one of their horses and wounded another. By this time some men were landed to the Major's assistance, and these with the first party behaved so well that the Militia retired to the face of a hill opposite to the ships, which fired some guns which reached so near them that they retired, and some did not draw bridle till they came to Paisley.'

"Having communicated the above to a worthy gentleman, who was present at this little scuffle, he is pleased to acquaint me, 'That the heritors of Renfrewshire, formed in a troop under the Lord Cochrane, at the council's appointment, were at this time keeping guard at Greenock. When Major Fullarton landed near the kirk of Greenock, John Houston younger of that Ilk, lieutenant of the troop, and Thomas Crawford of Crawfordsburn, eldest quartermaster to it, with some gentlemen in company, rode down towards Mr. Fullartoun and his men, who had put up a signal for parley; an Houstoun having expostulated with the Major on their invasion, he answered—'They were come to their native country for the preservation of the Protestant religion and liberties of their country, and it was a pity such brave gentlemen should appear against them in the service of a popish tyrant and usurper. Upon which Houston said he was a liar, and discharged his pistols amongst them, as did also the rest of the gentlemen with him, and the Major and his men returned their fire very briskly, but did no execution; only Houston's horse, being of mettle and unused with fire, threw him, but he soon remounted and returned to the troop.'

"Upon their flight Sir John with the rest came ashore and entered the town of Greenock, and endeavoured to prevail with the inhabitants to join in defence of religion and liberty. He seized about forty bolls of meal for the use of the army, and then, upon a false alarm, went off in the night and sailed back to Cowal, and then, too late, declared it was folly to attempt the Lowlands as yet, they being everywhere guarded with soldiers and militia."

The first vessel belonging to the port which crossed the Atlantic was in 1719 (part of the Darien expedition in 1697, having been fitted out from Cartsdyke), but shortly afterwards the shipping increased rapidly. About this time the rising prosperity of the place excited the jealousy of London, Liverpool, and Bristol to such an extent that they falsely accused the merchants of Greenock and Port-Glasgow of fraud against the revenue, first to the Commissioners and afterwards to the House of Commons. This was triumphantly refuted, and they were completely exonerated of all charges, and in spite of every effort to crush its infant commerce it went on amazingly. The first square-rigged vessel which was launched from our shores was in 1764, and was built by a Mr. Peter Love. The number and tonnage of vessels belonging to the port have been already given at page 56. The earliest trade seems to have been the Herring Fishing, and in the reign of Charles II., and under the patronage of the Duke of York, a Society of "Herring Fishers" was established on the Clyde, with particular privileges, In 1676 they enclosed a large piece of ground, which they called the Royal Closs. The Company was dissolved, and the buildings afterwards used as warehouses. The Herring Fishing has been continued by various individuals, and the quantity cured gives an average of about 19,000 barrels annually. An early branch of our commerce was in Tobacco, which was trans-shipped to the Continent, and in return other commodities were often taken in exchange. So far back as 1752, the Greenland Whale Fishing was carried on; it was, however, soon given up, but revived again in 1786, at which time there were three large ships employed in the trade; and though revived again at a later date may be now considered as abandoned—the last ship having been purchased by Captain Ross to accompany this enterprising individual in a voyage of discovery to the Pole. The most considerable trade which Greenock had, at an early period, was with America; this suffered a treat depression when that Colony waged war with the Mother Country, and it may be said to have gradually declined ever since. At present, however, Greenock has vessels trading to every part of the world, and from the average amount of duties received from the Customs at this port, it will be observed that trade is by no means falling off. The West and East Indian, and North American trades, may be considered at present as the principal. Newfoundland and South America have also employed a considerable number of shipping. The Coasting trade has rather declined since the introduction of steam in 1812, which facilitates the towing of small vessels to Glasgow against wind and tide.

This was the first port in the kingdom to petition against the Renewal of the East India Company's Charter. The inhabitants were first called together to take the subject into consideration in December, 1811. In 1812 a deputation was sent to London on this important business, and it is known that in 1813 a partial partici-pation in the trade was conceded to the outports. In Spring, 1816. the first ship from Scotland for the East Indies sailed from Green-ock. This vessel, the Earl of Buckinghamshire, Captain Christian, of 600 tons register, was soon followed by others, and the tonnage now embarked in the trade is very considerable; thus affording employment to ships when it was difficult to be found elsewhere, and from the duration and healthiness of the voyage forming an admirable nursery for seamen. It is to be hoped that ere long the trade to China will also be thrown open to the country at large, petitions to the legislature to this effect having lately flowed from every corner of the kingdom.

In a place like Greenock, which had so many shipping, it is to be expected that many fearful accidents would occur. The waste of individual life by drowning or falls from masts, etc., would make a long and melancholy catalogue. But, independent of this, vessels have been wrecked in our own channel, some have been burnt at sea, and others foundered on the deep or been cast away upon foreign lands. But, probably, the most melancholy intelligence which reached this port, was the loss of a number of our vessels on the coast of Portugal. The following are the particulars:—

Copy of a Letter from Captain Gibson, of the Robust, to the Owners here, dated 30 *leagues north of Lisbon,* 4th April, 1804.

"I am sorry to acquaint you of our melancholy misfortune, which happened on the morning of the 2d instant. At four o'clock we struck the ground, and drove on shore, and about thirty or one-and-thirty more of the fleet, and the Apollo, our Commodore. A great many lives were lost out of the several ships, and the sight is dismal to behold for many miles along shore. All our crew got on shore without the loss of a man. The Robust is all together, and fast; but the water ebbs and flows in the hold, and the surf is so heavy, rendering it impossible for any person to get now near to her; and I do not think anything belonging to her will be saved, as she will break up in a very short time, and don't expect her to hold fast till to-morrow morning. The accident was merely through neglect of the Commodore. As the wind was from the S.W., there was no occasion to stand so far to the eastward. All the fleet was sensible of being to the eastward, and some of them tacked, when he fired at them to bring them to: but he himself has suffered, with about 200 of his crew, some of whom were on the wreck these sixty hours without any subsistence. The Clyde ships which have suffered here are the Elizabeth, Galt; the Peggy, Carnochan; Peggy, Bartley; Active, M'Niccol; Fame, Gammel; Albion, M'Ewing; Nancy, Weir; Caledonia, Gilkison; and ourselves. We had much ado to get on shore, as no boat was able to stand the surf. There was a great deal of people lost out of the Clyde ships; some of them upwards of half their crews. There is a British Consul here at present, who came from a town about eight miles off, called Figueiro. I have nothing more to mention at the present time; but I will write you when I get clear of this, which I think will not be for some weeks, as we are to wait here, by order of the Consul, until we all get away together in a vessel to Lisbon."

During the war, privateers[1] and letters of marque, owned by Greenock merchants, were very successful, and a number of gallant exploits were performed by our seamen. The ships of war also occasionally visited the place, and, for a considerable time (on the remonstrance of the Magistrates), a guard ship was kept at the Tail of the Bank. The largest class of war vessels seen here was a 42 gun frigate, and one 74, or line-of-battleship, came up as far as Gourock. During a war they can be of little service stationed here, as the most effectual mode of protecting the trade, and also the town, is cruising in the channel and meeting the enemy before they reach our doors.

The Coasting trade, though it has diminished, as already mentioned, still gives employment to a number of men, and also to a fair amount of tonnage. The following is a statement for the years 1828 and 1829:—

Irish Coasting Trade.

---

1. Fourteen privateers were fitted out in three months when the American war broke out.

	INWARDS.		OUTWARDS.
1828,............208	26,325	147	19,110
1829,............443	26,451	250	32,750

Great Britain.

	INWARDS.		OUTWARDS.
1828,............443	39,990	577	51,605
1829,............520	44,018	554	54,000

About 50 years ago, though the Foreign and Coasting trade of the port had increased to a considerable extent, yet a distinct knowledge of the principles of navigation, for making the requisite observations for ascertaining the longitude by lunar observation, and the latitude by double altitudes of the sun, as practised in the East India trade, was but imperfectly known. Indeed, no shipmaster from the Clyde had then attempted to reduce it to practice, nor does it appear that any teacher in this country had possessed the requisite means to give instruction to seamen on this important branch. The shipmasters of the old school had an inveterate prejudice on this score, and consequently the rising generation were entirely deprived of the means of practical as well as theoretical knowledge. Fully aware of this branch of education to the trade, Mr. Lamont, shortly after his appointment in 1781, went to London for the express purpose of obtaining information on the subject, and also the requisite instruments, in order to prove to seamen the absolute truth of what they merely knew by report. It was during the magistracy of the late Roger Stewart, Esq., that an instrument was procured, for the twofold purpose of reducing to practice the principles of geometrical surveying, and for observing the contemporary bodies required in taking lunar distances by the sextant, which had been already procured by Mr. Lamont, as well as a pocket chronometer by the late John Melville. About 1789 or 1790 he also procured

Dolland's achromatic telescope for observing the eclipses of Jupiter's satellites, and a planetarium for illustrating the solar system, with its accompanying tellurian and lunarian complete. Thus provided, he was in a state for making actual observations for explaining the lunar theory, and fur emulating the Americans who then frequented the port, and who boasted of their superior knowledge in these matters. The first individual to whom British seamen are indebted for reducing the complete lunar theory to practice was the late Astronomer Royal, the Rev. Neville Maskelyne, who, after his voyage to Saint Helena in 1761, planned the Nautical Almanack, and the requisite table for its use. By others these have been brought to that degree of perfection necessary for the seaman's use. Since that period the famous Ramsden and Troughton have executed, under the patronage of government, their accurate and expeditious dividing engine, and produced the instruments required.

The first that availed himself of instruction on this subject, under Mr. Lamont, was a Mr. Robertson about 1788, who used the first metal sextant known on the Clyde, which was made by Jones of London. Mr. Troughton, after this, invented the light patent sextant, and also the circle of reflection, which has been proved to have been of unrivalled use in nautical astronomy. Captain James Hamilton, of the brig Nancy (cousin to the late Professor Hamilton of Oriental Languages), was the next who procured a sextant, in 1790, and prosecuted this study with much success.

Lieutenant-General Sir Thomas Brisbane (then Major Brisbane) was the first person who sailed from the Clyde with all the requisite instruments for ascertaining his situation at sea with anything like precision. He had several chronometers, a circular instrument by Troughton divided on gold, and a sextant by Dolland. He sailed from hence in the brig Fame, Captain Armour, in 1799. He, and the late Quintin Leitch, then Captain of the brig

Clyde, who became an early proficient in such observations, communicated by signal during the whole voyage, and through life a warm friendship existed between them. The late Captain John Udny was among the first who carried, at his own expense, books, instruments, etc., in a complete state for making lunar observation, and was allowed to have been the most expert lunarian then sailing. Since that time, however, every attention has been paid to this useful branch of education, and were it not that some might consider it invidious to notice by name many Captains who are an ornament to their profession, we would most cheerfully give them a place in this simple record. The fair fame they have earned is not the less remembered, and they may rest assured that thus trying to lessen the tedious monotony of a long sea voyage only endears them the more to those who intrust them with their property, as well as the lives of passengers and seamen. It is a situation of all others of deep responsibility. A ship on the ocean is to the master a little world quite under his own control; the happiness and comfort of all under him may be mainly attributable to him, and by his doing all in his power to form the mind of those youths intrusted to him, and by seconding the efforts of the teacher in giving useful information, he confers a greater honour on himself than on those who receive the boon. In this way there would be fewer run-aways from ships, while a wild boy would be generally awed into submission by treatment at once conciliating and kind.

*　　　*　　　*　　　*　　　*

Chapter 9.
LOCAL GOVERNMENT.

THE government of the town till 1751 might be considered as vested entirely in the hands of the lord of the manor, This year, as we have already stated, the first Magistrates were elected, and the origin of nine composing the Council was the continuance of the same number which superintended the receipt of the malt tax. Sir John, in the handsomest manner, vested all the right he possessed in the feuars and sub-feuars to elect their own rulers, and few places in Scotland have such an inestimable privilege. To our first Magistrates, etc., down to a late period, the inhabitants are under deep obligations. They watched with a parent's care the growing importance of the community; and it was not until about 1796 that bickerings were heard at our council table. This was revived again, in 1812 and at this period the first paper war commenced. The difference about the old Coffee Room revived party animosity, which has certainly not lessened, and the town is now divided into two distinct parties which are known as "Reds and Blues," The origin of this name arose from the magesterial contest in 1825, the one gentleman's coach-drivers having assumed the blue ribbon as a mark of distinction, and the others immediately decorated their hats with red. This contest lasted for six days when 497 votes were polled, and the Magistrates voted for by the Reds were elected by a majority of 15. It is to be regretted that party spirit does not rest with these elections, but has been often the means to convey strife and divisions into other societies and institutions, where this should have nothing to do. Every person should be allowed to express and hold his own opinions, without being held up to ridicule, or condemned for acting the part of every reasonable man, merely showing he has a mind of his own. The Magistrates hold courts every week in the Town Hall, independent of their giving attendance every day, to examine into cases connected with the police, etc.

Names of Magistrates, &c., for 1829.

*Bailies—*William Leitch and Robert Ewing.
Robert Baine, Treasurer.

Counsellors.

John Fairrie.	John Thomson.	John Miller.
Thomas Turner.	Robert Steel, jun.	Wm. Johnston.

Office-Bearers.

Alexander Dunlop, Esq., Advocate, Assessor for the Town, at Edinburgh.
John Patten, W. S., Law Agent, at Edinburgh, for do.
James Turner, Town Clerk.   J. K. Gray, Depute do.
Archibald Wilson, Deputy Treasurer.
John Davidson and George Williamson, Joint Procurators Fiscal.
George Hamilton, Superintendent of Public Works.
Andrew Stewart, Harbour and Dock Master.
Thomas Alexander, Collector of Harbour Rates.
James Dunn, Collector of Anchorage, Steam Boat Dues, &c.
Robert Lyle, Superintendent of Town Police.
John Campbell, Superintendent of Quay and Harbour Police.

There is also a Justice of Peace Court, at which the following Justices preside:—

Lt.-Gen. Dun. Darroch	Wm. M'Dowall.	John Denniston.
of Gourock.	The Sheriff Substitute.	Thomas Lang.
Capt. Duncan Darroch,	Alexander Dunlop.	James Likly.
yr. of do.	James Watt	Peter Hunter, jun.

Sir M. S. Stewart, Bart., M.P.
Capt. H. Stewart.
P. M. Stewart.
Robert Wallace.
Robert Steuart.
James Hunter.
Thomas Bissland.
David Crawford, D. C.

Hugh Crawford.
John Dunlop.
William Macfie.
James Oughterson.
James Leitch.
Alexander Graham.
Roger Aytoun.
John Buchanan.
Arch. M'Kinnon; Proc. Fiscal.

James Robertson.
G. Robertson.
A. M'Leish.

Bailies, ex-officiis.
William Leitch.
R. Ewing.

The Sheriff Court was established on the 27th January, 1815, and opened on the 3rd May following. It is held once a week during session, and oftener as occasionally required. In virtue of the Act of Parliament in 1825, the Sheriff holds a court for the recovery of small debts. The first Sheriff-Substitute was Claud Marshall, Esq., who was also appointed in June, 1815, to the Admiralty Court.

The following abstract of the Town's Receipt and Expenditure will serve as a contrast between the years 1785 and 1819:

Revenues of the Town of Greenock in 1785, exclusive of the Water Tax, Road Money and Tonnage on Shipping, viz.

New Church Rents,	£224 14 0
Breast Cellars (Rent augmented),	115 18 0
Royal Closs,	200 0 0
Sheds on the Quays,	5 0 0
Flesh Market,	65 0 0
Anchorage, Coal Barrel, Weights and Measures,	76 0 0
Tolling the Bell (averaged),	4 0 0
	£690 12 0

CHARGES ANNUALLY.

Minister's Stipends and Sacramental Elements,	£111 0 0
Master of the English School (now discontinued,)	20 0 0

Master of the Latin School, ... 15 0 0
Master of Writing, Arithmetic, &c. (a gratuity), ... 13 13 0
Interest on £920, borrowed at 5 per cent., ... 46 0 0
Shore Master's Salary, ... 16 0 0
Drummer's do., ... 6 0 0
Billet Master's do., ... 2 0 0
Robert Shannon, late Shore-Master (a pension), ... 15 0 0
Harbour Feu-duty, payable
to Sir Michael Shaw Stewart, ... 66 13 4
Do. do., payable to Lord Cathcart, ... 33 6 8
Robert Townsend, Clock Master, ... 2 0 0
William Henderson, Bellman, ... 2 0 0
Town Officers, for attending the Roup of Church Seats, 0 5 0
Deputy Treasurer's Salary, ... 15 0 0

Exclusive of Repairs,	£363	18	0
Surplus,	326	14	0
	£690	12	0

*Abstract Statement of Revenue and Ordinary Expenditure of the Town
Proper, from 1st Sept., 1818, till 1st Sept., 1819.*

RECEIPTS.

Anchorage, Shore Bay, and Ring Dues, received
at Collector's Office, ... £264 10 3
Do. do. received from John Shanks, Taxman of
Dues on small vessels, ... 164 0 6
Do. do. two-fifths of Harbour Dues from Steam
Boats, in lieu of Anchorage, ... 104 4 2

Total from Anchorages, &c, ... £532 14 11

Mid Parish Church, for Seats let, ... £254 8 0
Do. Ground Rent of Seats held by subscribers, ... 102 18 0

£357 6 0

Flesh Market Dues, from 1st to 25th Sept., 1818,......... 7 17 0
Do. do. from 25th Sept,, 1818, to 1st Sept., 1819,
for 1956 oxen and cows at 9d.,...................................... 73 7 0
Do. 152 hogs at 4d.,... 2 10 8
Do. 11,312 sheep, 1856 calves, and 1 goat,
together 13,169 at 2d., ... 109 14 10
Do. 6167 lambs at 1d,.. 25 13 11

                                                                  £219 3 5

Deduct George Robb's commission as
Clerk of Market, ... £21 2 8
Do. James Stewart, Officer of Market,.......................... 16 4 0
Do. for cleaning Market and
printing Rules, &c .... 1 10 6...... 38 17 2

Net Revenue of Market 180 6 3

Shops under the Town Hall 60 0 0

Proportion of the Public Office accomodation,
charged the Harbour 18 6 8
Do. charged the Water Fund,... 18 6 8
Do. charged the Tax Office, ... 10 0 0

                                                                  £46 13 4

This sum was not brought to the Town's credit
till the following year. £1130 7 2
Rent of Town Cellars and Offices
at East Quay-head,.. 215 0 0
Rent from Mrs. Mackie's School House
at Kilblain,... 90 0 0
Do. from Robert Kerr at do., ... 3 10 0

                                                                  £93 10 0

Rent of Library, ... 25 0 0

Rent of two Booths in Fish Market, its other
receipts being lifted by Taxman of Anchorage, ... 10 10 0
Lairs sold in new Burying Ground, ... 123 12 6
Deficiency of Receipts to meet the Expenditure, ... 262 18 7

                                                                £1860 18 3

OUTLAY.

Interest of Debt, gross amount £24,215
16s. at 5 per cent., ... £1210 15 9
Deduct interest received from Kelly Road,
£5110, at 5 per cent., ... £255 0 0
Do. do. at debit of Mid Parish, £1616,
at 5 per cent., ...   80 16 0
Do. do. Water Trust, £36 12s. 11d, at 5 per cent., ...   1 16 8
Do. do. cash in Renfrewshire Bank,
£1740, at 4 per cent., ...   69 12 0

                                                                     407 4 8

Interest after making the above deductions, ... £803 11 1
Gross amount of Feu Duties for Burying Grounds,
Church Grounds, Town Cellars, Town Hall, &c., ... £148 11 0
Deduct received from the Harbours, ... £37 13 2
Do. from Mr. Gammell, ...   5 16 8
Do. from A. Crawford's Heirs, ...   4 0 3
Do. Wilson & M'Lellan, ...   0 10 0
Do. M. Johnston, ...   0 10 0
Do. A. Fleming, ...   0 15 0
Do. Old Dock, ...   1 1 0
Do. Charged to Debit
of Mid Parish Church, ...2 17 6......   53 3 7
Amount of Feu Duties after the above deductions, ...   95 7 5

                                                                £898 18 6

Mid Parish Church, Minister's Stipend
and Communion expenses,...£295 0 0
Precentor £10, Bell-ringer £2 2s.,
regulating clock in church £1 1s....................................13 3 0
Interest of Debt, £1616, at 5 per cent., ...80 16 0
Feu Duty, Church and Manse,..2 17 6
Sundry repairs of windows, painting, &c.,.....................12 10 0
                                                                    ----
                                                                    404 6 6

Public Officers, viz., Town Clerk,....................................£83 6 8
Treasurer, £25—Treasurer's Assistant, £20,.................45 0 0
Master of Police, £50—Proportion
of Town Officers' Pay, £30 12s. 11d, ...86 12 11
Assessor, £10 10s.—Billet Master, £5, ...15 10 0
J. Heron for repairs on Town Clock, £4 4s.—
Bell ringer, £6 6s., ...10 10 0
J. Davidson and George Williamson,
Fiscals, salary, ...£30 0 0
For prosecutions, ...36 14 6

                                                                    £66 14 6
Deduct amount of Fines received,—25 9 6.................41 5 0

Total charge for Public Officers, ...282 4 7

School Master's salary, viz. Teacher of
Mathematics, ...30 0 0
Latin Teacher, £25, and School Rent, £25, ...50 0 0
                                                                    80 0 0
Stationery, Stamps, and Printing, ...40 15 6
Proportion of Coal and Candle for Public Offices, &c., 27 16 6
Fire Insurance Premiums on Town's Property,.............8 16 8
Sundry Tradesmen's Accounts for repairs
at roof, windows, &c,, of Town Cellars,
and other property, may average   118 0 0
                                                                    £1860 18 3

Independent of the magisterial control over the various funds, etc., there are a number of commissioners and trustees who act over the fund for paving, lighting, and bringing water, etc., into the town. The Act for regulating this body is on the most liberal terms, and it is impossible for any person to look altogether at the municipal government of Greenock without admiring the wisdom which dictated her laws, and also hoping fervently, in the beautiful language of Scripture, "that peace may dwell within her walls," and that a liberal and patriotic feeling may always actuate her councils.

*   *   *   *   *

Chapter 10.
LITERARY & FRIENDLY SOCIETIES.

THE progress of literature in Greenock has been much behind its other improvements, and though societies have been frequently formed for reading original essays, etc., as also for debating interesting and popular subjects, yet these have been but short-lived, and consequently their effects in forming the public mind of but little importance. The first literary society was commenced in 1792, and existed about eighteen months. In 1812 "The Society for encouraging Arts and Sciences" was established, and continued for about two years. In 1814 "The Literary and Philosophical Society" was instituted, and existed for about twelve months. On the ruins of this, however, another was established, under the same name, which existed for five years. In 1819 and 1820 two debating societies were begun, and ended the same year. At present Greenock possesses nothing in the shape of a literary and philosophical society. The only thing approaching to this is the "James Watt Club," instituted in 1813, and intended to do honour to the memory of the celebrated improver of the steam engine, who, it is well known, was a native of Greenock. The members hold their meetings in the James Watt Tavern, at the low west corner of William Street, and what renders this place doubly conspicuous is the fact that on this identical spot stood the house in which Mr. Watt was born. The members consist of gentlemen belonging to the town, and honorary members in other places. The meetings cannot be said to be for any particular object, as regards science or literature, as no subjects are brought forward farther than the social conversation of the day, and we believe all subjects of a political or theological nature are excluded, lest their introduction should tend to injure the harmony and kind feeling which have hitherto been their principal characteristic.

The want of literary societies must have had a blighting influence in making our soil so barren in men of letters, and, however some may scout the idea, yet past experience confirms the fact. Look to many of our first senators, and where was it that the powers, which afterwards drew forth admiration, were first conspicuously developed? Was it not amidst these assemblies? In answer to this, turn to the names of Pitt, Sheridan, Fox, and Curran. And Burns, the Bard of Nature, states that, in a society of this kind in Tarbolton, he first felt something like genius. The humble village of Crawfordsdyke has done more for literature than Greenock, though we are not to suppose that *Jean Adam* could have had any opportunity of catching the breath of inspiration from the source now alluded to. Her song of "There's nae luck aboot the hoose" is a fine composition; it is one of those lyrics which have immortality stamped upon them. Some friends of the poet Meikle very injudiciously attributed this as a production of his pen, because, forsooth, a copy was found in his own handwriting amongst his papers. So would many have given Lord Byron the credit for writing Wolfe's noble "Lines on the Burial of Sir John Moore," from the fact of Medwin having heard his Lordship recite them, and his having stated the belief, in his "Conversations," that they were his production. Both Meikle and Byron were rich enough in fame, and, from weighing every argument in favour of Jean Adam, she is as much entitled to be considered the author of this song, as Wolfe was as the writer of that beatiful ode. It is strange that many, like this poor female, have given but one single gem to the world, and that that stray effusion has borne their memory along the stream of time, while more ponderous works have sank for ever in its depths. Burns envied the author of "Keen blaws the wind o'er Donnocht head;" Lowe wrote almost nothing but "Mary's Dream;" Herbert

Knowles his "Lines in a Churchyard;" but the fact is so obvious that it is useless to go farther. As little is known of Jean Adam, perhaps the following biography may not be out of place:—

"Her father was a shipmaster in Cartsdyke, and she was born there about 1710. Her productions prove that her education must have comprehended reading and writing; she must have learned needlework too, for that was afterwards one of her sources of subsistence. Now, these three branches, though they may be thought a scanty education by people of the present age, really formed the whole course given to very respectable ladies in her time.

"She for some time supported herself by keeping a day-school in the town of Cartsdyke, and she was in the practice of giving her services occasionally at needlework in the neighbouring families. A talent for making verses, especially in a woman, would in those days naturally be looked upon with some degree of wonder by the inhabitants of the small town where the prodigy lived. Jean's verses were, therefore, much admired by her friends and acquaintances, and their flattery encouraged her to prosecute her favourite amusement and to neglect the more solid industry on which she ought to have depended for support. She collected her poems and had them published by subscription in a small duodecimo volume, printed at Glasgow by James Duncan in the year 1734. They are dedicated to the Laird of Cartsburn: their success does not seem to have been very great, for there is a list of subscribers prefixed amounting only to 123. In consequence of the disappointment she exported a large bale of the impression to Boston, in America, which was at that time the worst market in the world even for good poetry, and Jean's having no quality to attract the attention of the public remained unsold, and she missed the golden harvest that she had fondly anticipated.

"Poor Jean Adam laboured under a nervous sensibility to a great degree. It led her into very great extravagance of conduct, of which Mr. Cromek has collected the following instances:—One day she told her scholars that she would read one of Shakespeare's plays to them. She chose Othello, which she read with uncommon pathos, and at the end of it she was so affected that she fainted away. On another occasion she told her scholars, that having read Clarissa Harlowe, she felt such a deep interest in it and such reverence for the author, Mr. Richardson, that she had determined to walk to London to pay her personal respects to him. This romantic journey she actually performed in about six weeks, and then returned to her school at Cartsdyke.

"She was a very pious woman; she treated the children who attended her school with great tenderness, and she was much beloved by all of them. But her strange enthusiasm proved fatal to her comfort and respectability. Whether she gave up her school in a freak of extravagant adventure, or whether it dwindled away from her neglect of it, it does not appear, but for some time she led an unsettled life, wandering about and living upon the bounty of her friends. Some time after the year 1760 she came begging to the house of Mrs. Fullarton, who had formerly been her pupil, and though a little remaining pride made her at first refuse some articles of dress that were offered to her, yet she afterwards returned and accepted of them.

"Her end was such as might have been expected from the state of beggary to which she had been reduced, as the following extracts from the records of the Poor's House of Glasgow will show:—

'Glasgow, Town's Hospital, 2d April, 1765.

'Admit Jean Adam, a poor woman, a stranger in distress-for some time has she been wandering about; she came from Greenock, recommended by Baillies Gray and Millar.'

'Glasgow, Town's Hospital, 9th April, 1765.

'Jean Adam, the stranger, admitted on Tuesday the 2nd current, died on the following day, and buried at the house expense.'"[1]

In science, the only institution connected with Greenock is that established for mechanics in 1824. For the two first seasons it went on prosperously, but of late there has been a considerable

---

1. Apart from the above-mentioned song there has been little attention given to Jean Adam's work until recently. See "The Poems of Jean Adam" by Bill Overton in Womens Writing, Vol. 10, No. 3, 2003. The article contains a fairly comprehensive bibliography and can be read online at www.triangle.co.uk/wow/ —GP

lukewarmness on the part of those attending, and last winter the lectures were discontinued. In connection with this institution is an excellent library and a number of valuable philosophical instruments with apparatus for illustrating the subjects treated in the lectures. Those who have given lectures here were mostly natives of the place, or residing amongst us.

Greenock abounds with societies of all kinds, for the relief of those at home, and for sending aid to foreign countries. The first is the British and Foreign Bible Society, which has three different branches, or penny-week auxiliaries. There is a branch of the London Missionary Society; a Gaelic School Society; a Female Missionary Society; and one lately established, called the Home Mission; as also the Society for Aiding the Jews. There is, for the relief of distressed females, the Female Association; the Old Man's Friend Society; and one for aiding the Destitute Sick. Independent of these, there are a number of Trades Societies, which give aid to sick members; as also three Mason Lodges— viz., the Greenock Mount Stewart Kilwinning, No. 11;[1] the Greenock Mount Stewart Kilwinning, No. 111; and the Greenock St. John's, No. 176.

The character of the people of Greenock stands very high; the superior ranks are considered intelligent and well-bred, as well as kind and hospitable to strangers. The middle ranks are thought to be also well-informed, and to possess a pretty accurate knowledge of the events and literature of the day. James Hogg, the poet, has often acknowledged that Greenock was the first place in Scotland that received his works with a friendly feeling, and spread their fame abroad. The poet Burns, who was only once in

---

1. A branch of this Lodge was established at Aleppo by Mr. Drummond, his Majesty's Consul. This gentleman, who was a native of Cowal, had a veneration for what he calls "his beloved Greenock," which neither time nor change could ever efface.

Greenock, had the satisfaction of finding his works wherever he
went; and it is well-known that Greenock was the first place
which commemorated his birthday in Scotland. It was also the
first which commemorated the birthday of James Watt in the
United Kingdom. We have already spoken at considerable length
of the loyalty of the inhabitants. But it was a considerable sacrifice of religious feeling, which compelled them, on the 15th July,
1777, to cause the drum to beat through the town on a Sacrament
Sabbath,[1] for men to be enrolled for manning three privateers to
protect the trade. A writer in the Scots Magazine for September,
1777, thus alludes to this somewhat memorable fact:—

"In consequence of an express which was received on the 12th,
informing that several vessels have been taken by provincial privateers,
so stationed in the mouth of the river that nothing can pass them, as such
as attempt to run they sink,—the Council met yesterday, and have
resolved to fit out three vessels, one of 16, one of 14, and one of 12
guns; for which purpose a subscription paper was set agoing about
twelve o'clock, and about two o'clock, when it came to be observed by
Collector P——, with whom I was then in company, I observed no less
than £2900 subscribed for. A committee is appointed for superintending
the equipment, a commodore and captains are already named, and
though this be Sacrament Sunday, the drums are beating for seamen to
serve for one month only, by which time it is expected that government
will send armed vessels to clear the coast. About 100 sailors are already

---

1. Up to this period the Sacrament was dispensed but once a year, and
   then at such times as the parish minister thought convenient. In the
   March following, arrangements were made to have the Sacrament
   twice a-year, at the periods now in use; and this was done in order to
   meet the convenience of the farmers. Remonstrances have been
   lately made against the present time, March and August, in consequences of the number of vessels and the consequent delay which
   takes place. This should surely be attended to, as the commerce of
   the port should not suffer, when another time may be equally
   answerable to all.

enlisted, 660 stand of arms are come down from Dumbarton, and plenty of stores and ammunition. The vessels are already victualled, and the sailors appear so keen for the expedition that, in case of calm weather, they are taking plenty of oars on board."

A striking proof of the quietness of the inhabitants may be found in the fact of no military ever being stationed here, except when some emergency has called for their presence. It has been confessed, however, that when mobs have assembled in our streets, though this has been seldom, that they have partook much of the character of the "Porteous Mob" in Edinburgh,—determined for the time, but soon over. The most serious was the Sailors' Riot, of which the following account is given in the Scots Magazine for June, 1773:—

On Thursday, March 4,[1] a great number of sailors assembled at Greenock, and, in a riotous and disorderly manner, peremptorily insisted for an increase of their wages, which the merchants declined complying with, as they have already from four to five shillings per month more than what is given in any other port in Britain. The magistrates and several of the inhabitants were at the greatest pains to convince them of the impropriety of their conduct, and the bad consequences that might result from their persisting in it; notwithstanding which, they next day were more outrageous, and having obliged the rest of the sailors to join them they went on board all the outward bound

---

1. The following extraordinary fact occurred this same year:—A young man, in the seafaring way, named Black, to appearance died of a high fever a Greenock upon Tuesday, the 19th ult. He requested, on his bed, that the coffin should not be nailed close until his friends at Dunoon might see his corpse. His body was carried to Dunoon on Thursday following, and while a sister of his was kissing the corpse and taking the last farewell, to her surprise, as well as that of several spectators, he revived, called for a drink of water, which was immediately given him, and he continues in life and health ever since.

vessels, struck their topmasts, locked up the public sail-lofts, hindered the loading and unloading of any vessels, and put an entire stop to all manner of business at the port, parading the town in a hostile manner, and threatening and punishing such sailors as refused to join them. In order to assist the civil power in putting a stop to such illegal proceedings, two companies of the 15th Regiment marched from Glasgow for Greenock on Sunday morning, March 7th, and the same evening some of the inhabitants secured four of the ringleaders, and delivered them over to the custody of the military, who were immediately surrounded by a vast number of the sailors and most incessantly pelted with stones, bricks, etc. The magistrates again used their utmost efforts to prevail upon the mob to desist and disperse, but without effect, for they still continued throwing stones, bottles, etc., both at the magistrates and military, who were at last obliged, in their own defence, to fire, whereby two women were unluckily killed and a man and a woman wounded. The mob then gave way, but assembled again in greater numbers about nine o'clock, threatening to burn the houses of the magistrates and the ships in the harbour if the prisoners were not immediately delivered up to them, which was complied with. They were joined the next day by about two hundred sailors from Port Glasgow; after which they were still more daring, added new articles to their proposals, and refused to accept of their former demand. On this more military were applied for, and two troops of dragoons had arrived to assist in quelling the mob; but their assistance was unnecessary, for, by the activity of the grenadiers and light infantry of the 15th regiment, on Thursday, March 12th, above forty of the rioters were secured. Upon examination they were dismissed, excepting twenty-four, supposed to be the chief actors in the mob, and on Friday, the magistrates of Greenock, intended by the principal inhabitants, without any of the military, went out to such of the sailors as kept in a body; when the latter, observing that their behaviour was disagreeable to the townsmen, forthwith dispersed, and most of them returned to the respective ships they belonged to."

The Meal Mob, in 1785, showed much determination, though on this occasion the female part of the community were the principal actors.

Rather an unfavourable impression has been made on the minds of strangers as to the correct morals of the inhabitants, from the number of public-houses in our street, every third or fourth door, in many places, having to the name of the occupant this appendage—"licensed to deal in British and Foreign Spirits," and the number of licences annually granted for the town being, in 1825, 1228—and in 1829, 1116. The decrease on the number issued has arisen from tea and tobacco dealers having given up; as, on the whole, those granted to beer and spirit retailers increased.[1]

How far the imputation is correct, it is difficult to say, but if the lower orders did not give considerable encouragement to these places of resort, many of them would soon be abandoned. It is a pleasing trait, however, in the character of the inhabitants, that a due reverence is paid to the Sabbath, though probably this is not so much attended to as it was. Not many years ago it was impossible to walk the streets about nine o'clock, on the evening of that day, without hearing the "sound of praise from kindred roof," and the herring vessels[2] laying at our quays sent forth a similar sound of worship at the same hour.

The want of public works, or rather of cotton manufactories, has been much felt, as regards the rising generation. Boys are often found wandering about the streets and quays, and in many cases get into a careless, idle kind of life, which injures their future prospects. It is to be hoped that public works, through the means of the Shaws Water Company, will soon spring up

---

1. The only other duties collected by the Excise are on the manufactures of crystal, soap, etc.; and these appear, in 1825, to have been, along with the licenses, £21,242, and in 1829, £24,432.

2. A very inadequate idea can now be formed of these vessels which frequented the port: on the 17th June, 1775, no less than 73 vessels left the harbour for the fishing. Immense shoals of herrings were taken betwixt Greenock and Dumbarton, and at the mouth of the Gairloch.

amongst us and give employment, not only to them, but also to delicate females, who are unable to work at a more laborious occupation.

In common with most of the towns in this country Greenock has a Saving Bank, where the poor are enabled to lay up their earnings and keep them entire for some future emergency. By doing this, when sickness comes, they are not altogether unprovided, and thereby much money to be spent was put aside in this way, our poor's rates would soon diminish, the comforts of the people would be bettered, and our nation's best defence, viz. the ordinary classes, would take their stand, as once they did, as the pride and glory of our country.

*   *   *   *   *

Chapter 11.
SHIPBUILDING & MANUFACTURING.

IT has been stated by many that seaport towns are unfavourable for the encouragement of manufactures, except what merely belongs to the furnishing of ships and other stores connected with the sea. This assertion has been long exploded, and it only requires talent and enterprise to succeed as well here as any other place. The principal manufactures in the meantime, however, are, in a great measure, connected with the seafaring life.

Among the oldest establishments is the rope-work possessed by the Messrs. Ramsay, near the old battery. It was begun by Robert Donald in 1725, and was in different hands till purchased by its present possessors. Besides this, there is a variety of works, where excellent ropes of all kinds are manufactured. There is the Gourock Rope-work Co., as also Messrs. Quintin Leitch & Co., Messrs. M'Nab & Co., and some smaller works.

In connection with these, Messrs. Ramsay, and M'Nab & Co. manufacture sail-cloth, the latter of whom have erected a large mill for this purpose on one of the falls of the Shaws Water. The appearance of this building from the water near Gammell's Point (formerly known as Garvel Point) is very interesting.

Shipbuilding, from an early period, has been carried on with great success, but previous to the breaking out of the American war, almost all the large vessels belonging to the Clyde were built in America. Peter Love was the first in Greenock who built a square-rigged vessel; this took place in 1764: she was launched near the spot where Messrs. John M'Lellan & Co.'s counting-house is situated. Walter M'Kirdy built the next the same year; she was launched from the shore at the bottom of Charles Street.

Both of these vessels went to the West Indies. Shortly after, John Scott (father to the present Mr. Scott) built a large vessel for the town of Hull, most of the timber for building which was got from Hamilton. The building-yard of Messrs. Scott & Son is allowed to be the most complete in Britain, excepting those which belong to the Crown. It has a fine extent of front from West Quay to the termination of West Burn, and has a large dock, which was altered lately to the plan of the new dock. All the stores and different lofts are entirely walled in, and, independent of the building premises, they have an extensive manufactory of chain cables. The number of vessels launched from this place has been very great, but the largest ever built here, or in Scotland, was the Caledonian, of 650 tons, in 1794, for the purpose of supplying the Royal Navy with masts, etc.

Messrs. Steele & Carsewell began business at the Bay of Quick (formerly known as the Bay of Wick) in 1796. The first vessel built by them was the Clyde, commanded by the late Quintin Leitch. Mr. Carsewell took a branch of this business to Port-Glasgow, where he died in 1815, at which time the partnership was dissolved. During this copartnery they built 24 square-rigged vessels, and 11 fore-and-aft rigged vessels. One of the former class was the Bengal, which vessel was launched in February 1815, and was the first vessel built in Scotland for the East India trade. Messrs. Robert Steele & Co. entered the present premises[1] at the east of the town in 1816, and have built 30 square-rigged vessels, and 14 fore-and-aft-rigged vessels. In

---

1. In the same place, about fifty years ago, a Mr. Halliday had a building yard, and was succeeded by Alexander M'Kechnie; and David Porter and Mr. Morgan, Alexander M'Arthur and Mr. Munn had a building-place near the West Church; and, long prior to them, was Duncan Smith's building-yard at the Rue-end.

April, 1826, they launched the United Kingdom, which is the largest and most splendid steam-vessel built in this country.

Messrs. R. & A. Carsewell commenced in 1816 at the Bay of Quick. The first square-rigged vessel built by them was the brig Maria, and the largest launched there was the Clydesdale, of 584 tons.

Messrs. William Simons & Co. began in 1817 (near to R. Steele & Co.). The first vessel built by them was the brig Christiana, and the largest the ship Madras, of 550 tons. Since the time they commenced they have built 13 square-rigged vessels, 3 large steam-boats, and 5 fore-and-aft-rigged vessels. The whole tonnage of these vessels, British measurement, amounts to 5,220.

Messrs. M'Millan & Hunter's building-yard is situated still nearer the west. They lately built the brig Borealis.

Boat-building used to be carried on along with the other branches, but, for a number of years back, has been almost a separate branch. The boats of Mr. Thomas Niccol have been long famed, and the most of those which have won the prizes during the regatta races have been built by him. Mr. Niccol gives an accurate idea of the number of boats he has built, by mentioning that they would now reach about 24 miles in length. Mr. Nicol M'Nicol also carries on the same business with much success, and builds excellent boats.

Another prominent branch of our manufactures is sugar refining. This has been carried on with great success. The chief markets are Ireland, North America, and the Mediterranean. The situation of Greenock is peculiarly calculated for this business; the raw material being brought to the door direct. The following are the different houses employed, or that have been employed, in this trade:

The first sugarhouse built in Greenock stands at the foot of Sugarhouse Lane. It was built about the year 1765, by Mr. Mark

Kuhll,[1] for a company, of whom a part were gentlemen in Glasgow, and was an extensive undertaking for the time. It was enlarged in 1798, and is now the property of James Atherton, Esq., Liverpool.

The second sugarhouse was built, or rather a good substantial dwelling-house was altered to a sugarhouse, at the head of Sugar-house Lane, in the year 1788. The partners were all of Greenock. This house was also for two pans, and afterwards greatly enlarged, after being burned in the years 1793 and 1795. It is now the property of Messrs. M'Leish, Kayser & Co.

The third sugarhouse was built in 1802, in Bogle Street, by Messrs. Robert Macfie & Sons, for two pans. Enlarged to three pans in 1810.

Fourth sugarhouse—Built at Crawfordsdyke Bridge in 1809, by Messrs. John Fairrie & Co., and latterly greatly enlarged.

Fifth—Glebe Sugarhouse, built in 1811 or 1812, for two pans. Enlarged, and now the property of William Leitch & Co.

Sixth—Angus, Balderston & Co. built their sugarhouse near the High Bridge in 1826.

Seventh—Tasker, Young & Co. built their sugarhouse, as situated, on the last fall of the Shaws Water, east, in 1829.

James Fairrie & Co. first altered their sugarhouse to work on Howard's steam patent principle in 1819; and was the first in Scotland, and the second patent sugarhouse out of London. Since then, all the sugarhouses have been adapted to the patent process.

The straw-hat making has been carried on successfully in town, for a considerable time, by Messrs. James & Andrew Muir: and they have done much good in employing the young girls, and

---

1. The late John Gardner, sugar sampler, was bound apprentice to Mr. Kuhll for twenty-one years, fourteen of which he served, when he ran away from his bondage. Mr. K. used to say that he knew nothing of his business after his servitude; so great was the mystery in sugar refining at this period.

giving them habits of industry; while, by this means, the female part of the community have been often enabled to provide for aged parents, to assist poorer relations, and also to appear clean and genteelly dressed. Greenock is under deep obligations to these enterprising individuals, and the extent of the good they have done cannot be fully known. They commenced the manufacture of straw hats in 1808. The pipe-straw was sent from Bedfordshire to Orkney, where it was plaited; then sent to Greenock, and made into hats. This manufacture they still continue, and, in addition to which, they, in 1823, began the manufacture of Leghorn hats from rye-straw. In the following year they received from the Society of Arts, etc., Adelphi, London, "their silver Ceres-medal for specimens of plait in imitation of Leghorn;" and on the 19th May, same year, "their silver medal, or ten guineas at their option, for plait from British materials." In 1826, the Highland Society of Scotland voted them a silver medal, richly ornamented, and having in the centre the following inscription, in testimony of their approval of their exertions in the manufacture of Leghorn plait and bonnets:

Premium,

From the Highland Society of Scotland,
Adjudged to
MESSRS. JAMES & ANDREW MUIR,
Merchants in Greenock,
For having produced to the Society,
of their own manufacture,
The best specimens of Plait and Bonnets,
Made from Straw grown in Scotland,
And affording the closest imitation of the
LEGHORN BONNETS,
1826.

On 10th Dec. 1828, the Secretary of the Board of Trustees wrote them as follows:—"I have it now in my power to inform you, that you are allowed £28; being the premium of £14 offered for Article 31, and an extra premium of £14 added, on account of the extraordinary beauty and excellence of the manufacture.

(Signed)   "WM. ARBUTHNOT."[1]

The number of workers employed at the commencement was small; but it has annually increased, and may now be reckoned, in Orkney, at about 2000, and in Greenock, at from 200 to 300. In 1824, they invented light elastic waterproof silk hats on Leghorn bodies, which, for durability, lightness and elasticity, surpass any manufacture of silk hats that has yet been produced. These hats have met very general approbation, and have been well adapted for warm climates.

Manufactories for silk and felt hats are carried on to a considerable extent by A. & H. Patten, as also Blackadder & Orr. The articles produced by them and Messrs. Muir are considered equal to the finest English manufacture, and have even commanded a preference in the foreign market.

---

1. Two of the hats produced in Article 31 were the finest they have made, and had attached to them the following statement:—

Particulars of Miss Harrison's Bonnet, extracted from the Farmer's Journal:

Plait,..........121 yards.
Turnings,... 288,000
Stitches..... 286,000
Rows in an inch, 9 2-7ths.
Sold for 100 dollars.

Particulars of two Bonnets in Article 31, for competition before the Board of Trustees:

Plait,..........164 yards.
Turnings,....414,720
Stitches,.....410,500
Rows in an inch, 10.

By *Turnings*, is meant the number of straws in the edge of the plait; the *Stitches* are these turnings taken off by the thread.

The Clyde Pottery Co. was begun in 1816. They manufacture all kinds of goods, from the commonest to the finest tea and breakfast services. In connection with this, a mill was erected above Cartsdyke, for the purpose of grinding flints, etc., and they generally employ about seventy persons,

The Flint Glass-works were commenced about nearly the same period, and manufacture every description of crystal-work, both plain and fancy, which is considered equal in quality to anything done in Britain. They, as well as the Pottery, have an extensive foreign as well as home trade; and the latter supply every principal town in the country.

A most important branch, though but recently established here, is that of the manufacture of steam-engines, etc. Messrs. Scott, Sinclair & Co.'s is situated near Cartsburn House, and occupies a large space of ground: indeed, this work is considered as complete as any in the kingdom, and to the visitor has an interesting appearance. This work was first commenced by Burrow & Lawson, as a foundry, in 1791. It was bought by Wm. Brownlie in 1796 or 1797, and continued in his possession as such till purchased by the present proprietors in 1825. In the short period which has elapsed they have manufactured some splendid engines, and, what is more to be looked to than the appearance, they have wrought well. They have in hands the largest engine ever made, which is to consist of 200 horses' power, and is intended for a vessel building at Bristol. The number of men employed amount to about 220, while the weekly distribution of wages is £180.

A little farther east is a similar work, belonging to Messrs. Caird & Co. It was first begun as a foundry in 1809, and extended for the purpose of manufacturing machinery in 1826, This work is on almost a similar style of magnificence to the other, while the engines which have been made here are nothing inferior. They employ about 200 men; and consequently the amount of wages paid weekly cannot be far behind. To the stranger who has it in his power to visit these works, we can hardly imagine a finer treat. Every operation for producing that noble engine, which has done so much for this country, can be seen in a short time, from the most minute, up to the prodigious boiler, which gives life and animation to the whole. Two of the most splendid monuments which Greenock can ever rear to the memory of our illustrious townsman, James Watt, have been already completed; and no where can his unrivalled skill be seen to greater advantage than in the places now alluded to, which must have been the boyish haunt of those early days, when his mighty genius was breathing itself into existence.

There is an extensive Brewery[1] in Cartsdyke, possessed by Mr. James Watt (it originally belonged to a Mr. Knox), which is carried on to a great extent. There is also another brewery on a smaller scale, carried on by Messrs. M'Farlane & Rodger. The first brewery ever erected in Greenock was opposite Mr. Scott's building-yard, and here the inhabitants used to brew the beverage which, from the malt-tax imposed on every sack of malt, gave rise to our quays, and consequently to our present importance. Many a one has wondered how such a revenue could be produced at the early period of 1707, when the inhabitants were so limited, but this will cease to be a wonder, when we consider that little ardent spirits were then used, and ale was considered as almost an essential necessary of life. Our forefathers, in those days, discussed our burgh politics over this healthy but exhilarating draught, and, having parted from each other with all the kindli-

---

1. The first private brewery in Greenock was at the head of Sugarhouse Lane, nearly opposite Messrs. M'Leish & Kayser's sugarhouse. It was begun by Samuel Taylor but has been latterly employed as a soap work, a barm-work, and lastly as a bakehouse.

ness of neighbours, they, like honest Boniface, having "talked over their ale," retired in peace to "sleep over their ale."

It was not till of late years that Greenock possessed a distillery. The first that commenced was close by Mr. Hill's mill; another was begun near to the low west bridge; while another was carried on in Charles Street. But the most considerable was that erected in 1824, by John Dennistoun. This is allowed to be a complete work, while the spirit which has been produced has been pronounced of an excellent quality. About twelve months ago the Shaws water was introduced into the work, and has greatly improved the flavour of the spirit. Some idea may be formed of the extent of business, from the fact of upwards of £7000 being paid for duties annually.

Besides the mill[1] for grinding corn which is possessed by Mr. Hill, Mr. Thomas Fairrie has also an extensive building of the same kind, for the twofold purpose of grinding wheat and oats. Previous to the opening of the Shaws water, and to be ready for the first falling of this stream, the bakers of Greenock erected a mill for grinding their own flour. This was the first erection ever begun on this extensive undertaking, and to this spirited body the inhabitants are under deep obligations, for having set the laudable example of encouraging a company, whose future usefulness to the community at large can be but very inadequately appreciated.

Independent of the manufactures alluded to Greenock possesses a bottle-work, a chain cable-work, the extensive tan-works of Messrs. Park and Mr. Marshall, two soap and candle works, the steam saw mill, brass foundries, sail-lofts, and, among

---

1. The first erection of this kind in Greenock was the windmill which stood on the site of the late Mr. George Robertson's house. The old cotton mill, above Cartsdyke, was altered to a flour mill, while one for grinding corn is in the immediate neighbourhood. A place was also erected here for manufacturing of malleable iron from old scraps, etc.

other apothecary halls there is that of Mr. D. Brown, in Hamilton Street, where various chemical preparations of writing and durable inks, etc., have been most successfully carried on. A responsible person is kept here for the making up of medicines, the same as in Glasgow, Edinburgh, and London. The Messrs. Macfie, Lindsay & Co. have of late brought into great perfection the preservation of salmon, in a fresh state, capable of being kept for years, in every climate.

We had almost omitted to mention the existence of a business, which has been one of the earliest, and those engaged in which have done much good, in consequence of the number of men employed. We mean the coopers of Greenock, who carry on a most extensive trade, both in the foreign and home market; independent of those who make barrels for cured herrings, and are in some degree connected with the fishing. The most extensive are Messrs. John Buchanan & Co., Messrs. Baine, Mr. Robert Glass, Mr. William Chisholm, Messrs. Abram Lyle & Co., Mr. Robert Jamieson, and others. All the wine merchants have cooperages attached to their premises.

Printing, which was invented in 1430, and has done so much good in diffusing knowledge, was, till of late years, carried on here almost entirely in handbills, jobbing, etc. It was not till 1765 that any printer domiciled amongst us. This was a Mr. Macalpine, who was also the first bookseller. In 1802 the "Clyde Commercial List" was begun, and is still carried on by Mr. William Johnston. It is printed every Tuesday, Thursday, and Saturday. The same year the "Greenock Advertiser" was begun and was printed by J. Chalmers & Co. In 1817 the "Greenock Herald" was commenced by Mr. Mennons, but was discontinued, or rather merged into the "Advertiser," when Mr. Mennons became the proprietor in 1819. It is published every Tuesday and Friday. In 1827, when the rage for cheap papers was abroad, and when attempts were made to evade the stamp by printing them once a week under four different names, Greenock became possessed of one of these under the name of the "Independent." etc., but it was soon discontinued. Immediately after another paper was begun, entitled the "Greenock Iris," but, like its own name, became invisible in a few weeks. Mr. William Scott, late bookseller, who was also a printer, was the first who printed a book here:[1] this was "Hutcheson's Dissertation" in 1810, "Fisher's Catechism" in 1812, and two editions of "Hervey's Meditations" in 1813 and 1816. Mr. Mennon has since produced a number of elegant volumes. The first book printed by him was the "Literary Coronal" in 1821, which has been continued, and been followed by many other works, original and selected, all of which have been well received by the public.

Many of the manufactures which we have had occasion to mention are but of recent date. And though Greenock may be said to be chiefly dependent on her shipping, yet she cannot be too soon considered less so, and more dependent on her own resources; while, at the same time, it will make the shipping as much obligated in entering the port as we can be to them. Our sugarhouses, for instance, employ an immense tonnage in carrying the raw and refined material. It is in consequence of Liverpool being, as it were, the centre of an extensive manufacturing district, that she has risen to her present height of prosperity. It will be long ere we can attempt to rival this thriving city, but capital, skill, and enterprise, connected with the powerful aid of the Shaws water, will accomplish more, and in less time, than many imagine. This work is going on slowly, but surely, and has accomplished a great deal in the short period that has elapsed since its completion. From it the town and public works can have an excellent supply of water, the pipes being laid along our streets

---

1. See, Introduction, page V.

and lanes to both extremities of the town, as well as through the policy.

*   *   *   *   *

Chapter 12.
THE SHAWS WATER COMPANY.

BEFORE proceeding further, it may be as well to give some account of a work which has been the admiration of some of the most scientific men of the age.

The deficiency of water had been long a subject of complaint in Greenock, and in dry seasons, it had to be carted for the supply of the inhabitants from a considerable distance. Many attempts were made with the desire of remedying this, but until the establishment of the Shaws Water Co. nothing of importance was effected. Mr. Rennie made a survey, and increased the supply a little, by erecting a small reservoir near the town, but it was usually exhausted by two or three weeks of dry weather. About forty years ago, the late Mr. Watt, accompanied by the late Mr. George Robertson, also walked over the whole neighbouring grounds, and gave it as his opinion that nothing could be done but by small reservoirs, such as that afterwards made by Mr. Rennie. It appeared to Mr. Thom[1] of Rothsay, however, that by turning

---

1. In justice to a public-spirited gentleman, it may be proper here to mention certain circumstances in connection with the origin of the undertaking. "In 1820, when coursing together in Bute, and passing some of the aqueducts, Mr. George Robertson mentioned to Mr. Thom the great scarcity of water in Greenock, and asked if he thought a supply could be procured for it in the same way he had obtained the supply for the Rothsay Mills. Mr. Thom replied that he had no doubt but something in that way might be done; and asked Mr. Robertson respecting the various streams in the vicinity of Greenock. Mr. Robertson explained as to these, and mentioned particularly the Shaws Water and its localities: from which Mr. Thom

*CONT'D: [1]

the source of the Shaws water and other streams in the hills behind, and constructing reservoirs and aqueducts, the town might be plentifully supplied with water, but the attempt was by many pronounced impracticable, without raising it over the hills by force of steam. In 1824 he prepared a report, in which he stated it not only practicable to procure a supply sufficient for the inhabitants, but also to impel machinery, to an extent at least equal to what is impelled by steam in and about Glasgow. In consequence of this a company was immediately formed, and incorporated by Act of Parliament, under the name of "The Shaws Water Company," with a capital of £31,000 sterling.

For the information of those at a distance, as also of others interested, we subjoin a plan of the whole. The description which now follows, showing the present state of the works and their

---

1.   inferred that this stream might be carried to Greenock, and said so to Mr. Robertson at the time. "Mr. Robertson having mentioned this to some of his friends, and particularly to Sir M. S. Stewart, Mr. Thom was applied to in 1821 to inspect the ground and streams in the vicinity of Greenock, to ascertain the practicability of procuring the necessary supply. But Mr. Thom, being much occupied by the water and other operations at Rothsay mills, could not then afford the necessary time, on which account some other engineers were employed, who reported that the scheme was impracticable. Early in 1824 Mr. Thom was again applied to, and the operations at Rothsay mills being then brought near to a close, he made the survey accordingly and gave in a Report. Until Mr. Thom had finished this survey, however, no one had the least idea of anything beyond an ordinary supply for Greenock, save Mr. Robertson but on the first day of this survey Mr. Thom communicated to him, confidentially, what was likely to be the result of their first conversation on this subject. When, therefore, the Report appeared. every one was taken by surprise; some were equally astonished and delighted with the prospect, but most were disposed to treat it as a dream. The result is now well known."

capability of further extension, is from a pamphlet entitled "Account of Shaws Water," etc.

"The compensation reservoir, the auxiliary reservoir No. 3, the main aqueduct (something more than six miles in length), and the eastern line of mill leads, were finished early in April 1827, and on the 16th day of that month the water, from the great reservoir, was brought along the aqueduct, and down this eastern line to the Baker's Mill; which has ever since been supplied at the rate of twelve hundred cubic feet per minute for twelve hours in the day, agreeably to the regulations. Other three mill sites have also been feued on this line, and the necessary erections are in a considerable state of forwardness.

The embankment of the great reservoir, which is 60 feet high from the bottom of the rivulet, is now finished.

This reservoir contains two hundred and eighty-four millions, six hundred and seventy-eight thousand, five hundred and fifty (284,678,550) cubic feet of water, and covers two hundred and ninety-four and three-fourths imperial acres of land.

The compensation reservoir contains fourteen millions, four hundred and sixty-five thousand, eight hundred and ninety-eight (14,465,898) cubic feet of water, and covers about forty imperial acres. Its embankment is 23 feet high from the bottom of the rivulet.

The auxiliary reservoir, No. 3, contains four millions, six hundred and fifty-two thousand, seven hundred and seventy-five (4,652,775) cubic feet of water, and covers about ten imperial acres.

The other auxiliary reservoirs, Nos. 1, 2, 4, 5, and 6, are now about to be formed, and will contain something more than six millions cubic feet of water.

"Thus, the reservoirs already formed contain three hundred and three millions, seven hundred and ninety-seven thousand, two hundred and twenty-three (303,797,223) cubic feet, and when the other five auxiliary reservoirs are finished, the whole will contain above three hundred and ten millions (310,000,000) cubic feet of water.

"The whole annual supply, originally estimated, was six hundred millions (600,000,000) cubic feet. The Company have stipulated to supply the east line of mills with twelve hundred (1200) cubic feet per minute, for three hundred and ten days (of twelve hours each) in the year, and it is intended to give an equal supply to the west line. This will amount to five hundred and thirty-five millions, six hundred and eighty thousand (535,680,000) cubic feet annually. Taking the population of Greenock at 25,000, and allowing for each individual two cubic feet a day, this will require eighteen millions, two hundred and fifty thousand cubic feet annually, which leaves, of the original six hundred millions forty-five millions, seventy thousand (45,070,000) cubic feet annually for the public works and other purposes.

"The available drainage into the various reservoirs now formed is above seven hundred millions of cubic feet annually, and it will be observed that the reservoirs are capable of containing a full supply for the whole consumpt for more than six months; so that not only the surplus waters of one wet season may be retained for supplying the dry season of the same year, but the surplus of several wet years stored up to supply a drought of several years duration, should ever such occur.— *Any doubt of a full supply of water, at all times and in all seasons, to an extent much beyond what has been stipulated for by the Company, is altogether out of the question.*

The water for the supply of the *inhabitants, sugar works,* and others requiring *pure* water, is collected into reservoirs, *set apart for that purpose,* and as little as may be of moss water admitted into them. A separate aqueduct has also been made to carry this water to the filters, just above the town, where a basin has also been made large enough to contain something more than a day's supply of the filtered water. This aqueduct, which is fully fifteen inches square, is perfectly water-tight, being formed with stone, nicely joined and cemented, and costs something less than one third the price of a cast iron pipe of equal capacity. Wherever the pressure is not great, such a conduit is preferable to an iron pipe, as the water, by passing over stone, is rather improved than injured, which is not the case with iron. In this aqueduct (which is deep enough in the earth to avoid the frost of winter and the heat of summer) cesspools are formed for the deposit of sediment, it being desirable that the water should be as pure as the nature of things will permit before it enters the filters.

Three filters are now formed—each is fifty feet long, twelve wide, and eight deep. The water is made to percolate through them, either upwards or downwards, at pleasure. When it percolates downwards, and the supply of filtered water becomes sensibly less—which, after some time, must happen to every filter, by the lodgement of sediment—then, by shutting one sluice and opening another, the water is made to pass upwards with considerable force, and carrying the sediment along with it, falls into a waste drain made for that purpose. When the lodged sediment is thus removed and the water becomes clear, the direction of the sluices is again changed and the filter operates as before.

If the water usually percolates upwards, then, as before, when the quantity of filtered water falls short, one sluice is shut and another opened, and the water, passing downwards with considerable force, carries the sediment along with it into the waste drain. In either case the sediment is removed, and the filter again at work in less than an hour. This much sought for desideratum in filters has, therefore, at last been found, and Greenock is now supplied with abundance of pure water, at the very low rate of 6d. the pound of rental, being only half the price paid in Edinburgh and Glasgow.

"The water is carried, by an aqueduct, from the river and reservoirs, to a populous seaport town, with a redundant unemployed population, where roads, harbours, piers, and everything requisite for the most extensive trade and manufacture are already formed. Besides, by thus forming artificial waterfalls on advantageous grounds, every inch of fall, from the river or reservoir to the sea, is thus rendered available. In the present case a fall of 512 feet has been made available, of which not more than 20 was formerly occupied, or thought capable of being usefully employed. But, besides the immense advantage thus gained by increasing the fall, a still greater advantage is obtained from the greatly increased and perfectly uniform supply of water.

"It has already been stated that the reservoirs have been made so capacious as to contain a full supply for the whole works for six months, which enables the surplus of wet years to be retained to supply the deficiency of those that are dry, and it will be seen, by the following description, that these reservoirs, aqueducts, basins, and self-acting sluices turn to account every drop of water that flows from the whole drainage, during even the greatest floods; whereas, by former plans, a very large portion of these floods was allowed to run wastefully to the sea."

The various self-acting sluices, which are nine in number, have been all contrived or invented by the ingenious Mr. Thom, Civil Engineer, Rothsay. All we can do is merely to notice, by naming the various sluices, and referring for farther particulars to the pamphlet already alluded to. Those who have had an opportunity of seeing them in operation must admire the simplicity and ease with which this immense body of water is regulated. Many may still remember the devastation which was caused by the bursting of the dam above Cartsdyke, on the 15th March, 1815, when the stream, in its resistless course, carried everything before it, till it almost flooded the whole of Cartsdyke. Here this cannot occur, for the body of water is so kept in check, through the various self-acting sluices, that during the stormiest night, and should the "rains fall as it were their last," in silence and loneliness they would act on, with that safety and precision which gives security to the district where the various embankments have been made.

"THE LEVER SLUICE.—This apparatus, when placed on a reservoir that supplies any canal, mill, or other work with water (where the aqueduct between the reservoir and such work is on a level), will always open of its own accord, and let down the quantity of water wanted by such work, and no more; so that it not only supersedes a water-man, but also saves a good deal of water.

"THE WATER SLUICE.—This sluice, when placed upon the embankment of any river, canal, reservoir, or collection of water, prevents the water within the embankment from rising above the height we choose to assign to it; for whenever it rises to that height, the sluice opens and passes the extra water; and whenever that extra water is passed, it shuts again, so that, while it saves the banks at all times from overflow, it never wastes any water we wish to retain.

"THE DOUBLE VALVE SLUICE.—This apparatus answers the same purpose as the lever sluice, but is more applicable in cases where the reservoir is deep, and the embankment consequently large. It acts also as a water sluice, by opening and passing the extra water whenever it passes in the reservoir the least above the height assigned, and thereby supersedes a bye-lead.

In making hydraulic experiments, it will also be found of considerable importance; as, by keeping the surface of the water in the cistern, from which we draw water for the experiments, always exactly at the same height, it not only saves intricate calculations, but renders the result, upon the whole, more correct.

"THE SINGLE VALVE SLUICE.—The construction of this apparatus is, in some respects, similar to the double valve sluice; but its application is to situations where the reservoir is on high grounds, and where the water has to pass down a declivity before it is applied as a power to the mills.

"THE CHAIN SLUICE.—This apparatus answers exactly the same purpose as the last; only the construction is different.

"THE DOUBLE WEATHER SLUICES.—This apparatus is so far similar to the last described; but it has a double operation, the sluices first opening, one after another, as the streams increase, until they reach a given height; and then shutting, one after another, as they continue to rise above that height. Again, when the streams begin to fall, the sluices open, one after another, until they (the streams) fall to a certain point; and then again shut, one after another, as they continue to fall below that point; the same continuous rise in the streams first opening, and then shutting, all these sluices in succession; and, in like manner, the same continuous fall first opening, and then shutting, them in succession.

"THE SINGLE WEATHER SLUICE.—One of the purposes to which this apparatus is applicable, is to regulate the supply of water between a reservoir and mill, or other works, where the former is at a great distance from, and high above, the latter; where several streams fall into the aqueduct between them; and where the adoption of apparatus might be considered too expensive. But it may also be applied to several other useful purposes, as will readily occur to such as may have occasion to adopt it."

Before leaving the subject, we have only to remark, that to Mr.
Thom Greenock is under a debt of gratitude. This enterprising,
and, we may say, highly talented individual, has changed as it
were the face of nature; and where a comparatively barren hill
reared its head, life, animation, and cultivation are to be seen. For
ages the stream sought a different channel, and poured itself into
the Clyde near Ardgowan. In the short period of two years its
course was entirely changed; a little lake formed between the
hills; and the various streams which form this "Caspian" are
brought along the brow of the hill, till they reach Everton, and
from thence run off as circumstances may require. All this has
been done by a gentleman at once modest and intelligent; but to
allude to his talents, we have only to point to the Shaws Water,
which will make his name remembered while the stream itself
continues to exist.

In conclusion, we copy from the "Greenock Advertiser," of
the 17th April, 1827, the following interesting account of the
opening of the Shaws Water Aqueduct, which took place on the
previous day;—

"The 16th of April, 1827, will long remain a memorable day in the
annals of Greenock, Rapid as was its advance from the obscurity of a
fishing village to the consideration which belongs to the first seaport in
Scotland, we trust it is destined from this day to exhibit a still more
rapid progress as a manufacturing town, for which it has acquired facilities it did not before possess—and, we may add, which no place in the
United Kingdom now possesses in the same eminent degree.

"To form an immense artificial lake, in the bosom of the neighbouring alpine regions, and lead its liquid treasure along the mountain
summits, at an elevation of more than 500 feet above the level of the
sea, till, in the immediate vicinity of the town, it should be made to pour
down a resistless torrent, in successive falls, for the impelling of
machinery to a vast extent—this, in a few words, was the magnificent
conception of Mr. Thom; and never, probably, did the first trial of so

novel and extensive an undertaking demonstrate its capability and entire adaptation to its purpose, or excite such unalloyed and universal gratification.

"By the activity of Mr. James Thom, the engineer of the Shaws Water Company, all the preparations were completed, to admit of the water flowing from the great reservoir the whole length of the aqueduct, a distance of 6 miles; and yesterday, precisely at a quarter to twelve, the sluices were raised by our chief Magistrate, William Leitch, Esq., who immediately thereafter entered a boat prepared for the purpose, gaily decorated with flags, and was floated along on the first tide of the stream in its new and artificial channel. The spectacle of a vessel skirting the mountain's brow, and tracking the sinuosities of the alpine chain at so great an elevation, seemed the realization of a dream of the wildest fancy, and the course of the boat was followed by crowds of delighted spectators. It arrived at Everton, in the vicinity of the town, exactly at a quarter to three, where it was received with cheers and a salute of cannon. The water was then allowed to flow into the regulating basin for three-quarters of an hour. It is at this point that the stream takes its descending course, and a sufficiency of water having been poured into the basin, at half-past three the sluice was opened by Sir Michael Shaw Stewart, and the torrent bounded down each successive fall, and rolled along the alternate levels, with fearful activity. It was at this juncture that the scene became one of the most interesting and animated description. The spectators, who amounted to several thousands, but who had previously been scattered irregularly over a considerable extent of the aqueduct line, now became more condensed, and moved onwards as if in procession, following the march of the stream. In the appearance of the aqueduct a complete change had now taken place. What, a few minutes before, was a dry and unmeaning channel, exhibited now an impetuous torrent; by turns a cascade sending up clouds of spray and a swift-rolling current, seeking its unquiet course towards the Clyde, whose ample waters lay far beneath. Arriving at length at one of the lowest falls, on which the new Flour Mills belonging to the Society of Bakers have been erected, the Shaws Water no longer disported itself idly and in vain. The dizzying wheel was set in motion, with the fine machinery of the mills, and added new life to the scene. A discharge of cannon announced this event also. The mills and granary are on an extensive scale, and the former are driven by a water power equal to twenty-eight horses. The machinery, which has been constructed by Mr. John Wood, engineer, is remarkably fine, and by competent judges is pronounced inferior to nothing of the kind in Scotland. At half-past four the Shaws Water, which for ages had discharged itself into the Clyde at Innerkip, now terminated its easterly course in the river above this town. "In conclusion, we cannot help remarking, as a most singular circumstance, that the birth-place of Watt should have become the theatre for exhibiting the earliest practical demonstrations, on an extensive scale, of a great mechanical power, rivalling the utility of his own, and been the means of adding another name to the bright record of ingenious men, who have proved at once the benefactors of their country and of mankind."

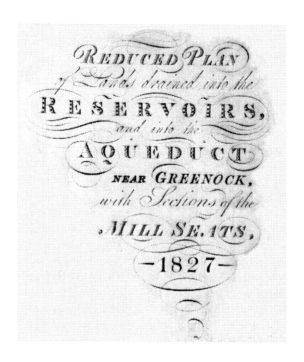

Surveyed by J. Flint & J. Linn as directed by R. Thom

Scale of Plan 80 Chains to a Mile.

0   10   20   30   40   50   60   70

Scale applies to maps 2, 3 and 4 only.

REFERENCE.

	Impl. Acres.
Ground, the Waters of which are drained into the Great Reservoir	3600.76
Ground drained by the Compensation Reservoir	344.08
Ground drained by the stream for regulating the Weather sluices	81.65
Ground drained by the Aqueduct	955.98
Total	**4982.47**

WATER.

	Acres.
Great Reservoir	296.729
Compensation Res.r	40.534
Aqueduct & Whinhill Res.	21.797
Reservoir No 3 with proposed ones Nos 1,2,4,5, & 6, and Catch Water drains.	37.505
Total	**396.565**

Map 1: overall outline of scheme.

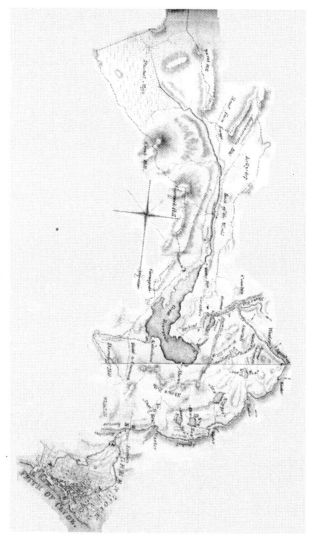

Map 2

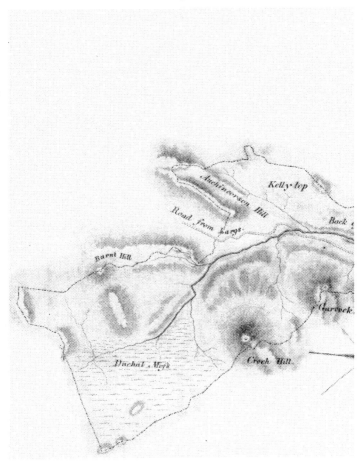

Map 3

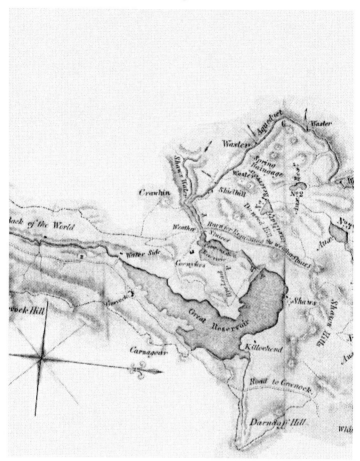

Map 4

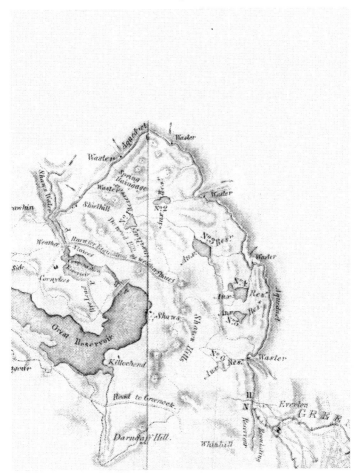

Map 5

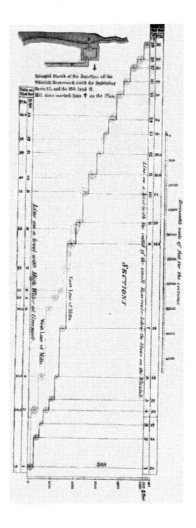

Plan of sections of the mill seats.

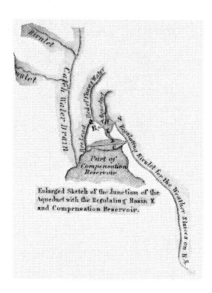

Enlarged Sketch of the Junction of the
Aqueduct with the Regulating Basin X
and Compensation Reservoir.

P G R. the Aqueduct
between 6 & 7 miles long.
N O X. East line of Mill Leads.
O Y. West line of Mill Leads.

*   *   *   *   *

Chapter 13.
WALKS & VIEWS.

THE walks about the place are unequalled in the vicinity of any other town in Europe, and they may be had of any length. The traveller may have mountain saunterings or level rides in different directions, and without almost ever losing sight of at least some peep of the beautiful and picturesque scenery of the Clyde. Although from no point in the neighbourhood can the stranger be disappointed of a charming prospect, perhaps the best is from the banks of the Shaws Water Canal, which has a most inviting level footpath, all along from its source at Loch Thom (or what has been called the little Caspian) to its termination. From it any person of taste, should he walk along it, will derive a high degree of gratification. He may ascend by the zig-zag line given to it by the Deling Burn, for the accommodation of the mill falls; and, as he moves upward, and is made acquainted with the whole design, he will become in some measure interested in the speculation, and not withhold his tribute of admiration of the suggestion that first led to the accomplishment of so magnificent an undertaking, by enterprising individuals, in concert with the lord of the manor.

Who could have supposed that a water, apparently not at all having such an elevation, and stealing along, in its lonely path, through a mossy wild, at the back of a rugged range of hills, scarcely known but to the solitary angler, could be brought to glide six or seven miles gently along their edge, and to pour down, from its heathery elevation of 600 feet, so many powerful and foaming cascades?

When he has got above the mill stations, and entered upon the path, the fascinating panorama will then be seen spread out before him in all its varied grandeur, and cannot fail to arrest his attention. On the east, his eye will be carried far away up through the channel of the Clyde, over an interesting landscape, till it is lost in the aerial perspective of the sky. Sweeping it nearer on each side, the broken descent of the land in many places, which are enriched with woods and gentlemen's villas, slopes to the edge of the river, and offers many beautiful sketches to the pencil. Port-Glasgow and Greenock on one side, and Dumbuck, with the ancient town and fortress of Dumbarton, on the other, will particularly attract his notice. But, as he carries the eye northward, it is met by the endings of the Grampian chain, where Benlomond and Benledi, with others less high, become conspicuous objects, and give a peculiar interest to the scene. As he moves westward again the tumultuous grandeur of the Argyleshire mountains present themselves in all their highland majesty. Here and there the different lochs are seen shooting away up among them, and from their shining surfaces reflect their dark shadows, which, to those unaccustomed to such romantic prospects, must be peculiarly pleasing. As he turns southward, the land is seen to flatten in many parts, and to break into points and islands, diversifying the picture. All the way downward, the mind, if indulging in reflections on the active pursuits of man, will find much entertainment on seeing so many vessels, of all sizes, pursuing their various courses on the water, from above Dumbarton till where Ailsa is seen far, far away, like a solitary watch-tower guarding the entrance of the Clyde; and here and there the steam-vessels make their

> "Circling paddles ply,
> And send their smoky pennants through the sky."

A very agreeable and picturesque walk turns to the right at the low Innerkip toll-bar; and, after ascending to the elevation above Caddel Hill, the residence of Alexander Thomson, Esq., it commands a beautiful prospect. Immediately below, and on a fine rising ground, stands Mr. Heron's Observatory,[1] which was erected in 1819, for the purpose of accurately finding the time. This was in some measure indispensable, for as chronometers were becoming more generally in use among the Clyde navigators than heretofore, it consequently became a matter of importance to have a suitable building, with proper instruments, in order that the rate of going of these valuable machines might be determined in the most perfect manner. Considering this erection to be an object of public utility, and immediately connected with the commercial interests of the port, the late Sir Michael Shaw Stewart granted to Mr. Heron a suitable piece of ground, free of the customary feu-duty, and subject to only a small rent.

The building is of an oblong octagonal form, and has two apartments. The eastern one is the observing room, in the middle of which stands one of the pillars that formerly supported the ancient West Quay Shade, but which now carries a transit instrument. Besides the transit and a circle—both made by that unrivalled artist, Troughton—the observing-room contains a sidereal regulator; a three-and-a-half feet achromatic and a six feet Newtonian telescope; a comet glass, wind dial, and all the usual appurtenances of a properly furnished observatory. The regulator has an escapement of a peculiar construction, which, as

1. The first observatory in Greenock was erected behind the Mid Parish Church, and contains the requisite instruments fur observation, etc. This place has been used as such by Mr. Colin Lamont, a highly meritorious gentleman, who was the first teacher of navigation in Greenock. Mr. Ryder and Mr. Lyon are the present teachers of navigation, and are highly creditable for their theoretic as well as practical knowledge of this branch of education. Besides the observatories now alluded to, Mr. Clark, watchmaker, has erected a place in Cathcart Street, behind his shop, which, with a transit and astronomical clock, answers very well for the regulating of chronometers.

it offers no resistance to the ascent of the pendulum, may be reckoned perfectly detached. Our celebrated townsman, James Watt, when he last visited Greenock, examined it, and pronounced it to be different from any he had seen. The western apartment is occupied as a library and sitting-room.

The building was scarcely completed when the comet of 1819, which excited so much attention, appeared. Observations were made here on it as early as at the great observatories of Europe. These were continued as long as it was visible, and the results appeared from time to time in our local journal. Since then the ordinary work of the observatory has been carried on with little interruption.

It has been acknowledged by every traveller who has visited Greenock, that for varied beauty of scenery it is almost unparalleled. There is not a height in the suburbs that does not afford a panoramic view of such a character as to call forth the admiration of every one not absolutely dead to the lovely picturing of nature. Accordingly, the observatory, being placed on an eminence at the south-west quarter of the town, commands a prospect in the highest degree interesting; and of which some idea may be formed from the annexed view, taken by an artist not insensible to the beauty which he has delineated. On leaving the observatory, and walking along the ridge of hill till above Gourock, the prospect widens and varies at every half mile. It is never seen to such advantage as at the close of the day, when the descending sun brightens and gilds the ridges of hill on the opposite side, as with a stream of gold. You are particularly struck with the pointed hill known as Benarthur, or the Cobbler, which rises near to Arrochar; and, stretching away further to the west, the Duke's Bowling Green is exceedingly marked. But the most majestic of all is the high and noble-looking hill which divides Lochgoil from Lochlong. This hill can be seen at an immense distance, and can be distinctly observed from Arthur's Seat and Edinburgh Castle.

Looking further down, the shores of Cowal, with their heath-brown hills, darken the atmosphere; while Dunoon and Bute are distinctly visible. But the prospect---which is here seen in all the variety of mountain, lake, and river is at once bounded by the huge hills of Arran, which seem standing in sullen grandeur, gazing on the beautiful scene.

Another delightful and no less varied walk, commences about the spot where the frontispiece, or eastern view of Greenock, is taken. In ascending the hill, in almost a direct line, all that we have already stated can be seen. But the prospect becomes more ample as regards the scenes up the Clyde. On reaching Corlic top, the view is truly enchanting; and though only 800 feet above the level of the sea, gives an exceedingly fine outline of the hill of Ardmore, Gareloch, Lochlong, and all the surrounding objects. Going farther back there is a hill, the top of which is called Prospect Point, and from this elevation portions of the shires of Lanark, Dumbarton, Stirling, Argyle, Ayr, and Bute, while the waters of Lochlomond, and part of one of her many fine islands can be seen. To direct the traveller to every object worthy of regard would be tedious; and he must be cold of soul who can range along the hills of Greenock, without being more than struck with the glorious sight which every where opens upon him. The lover of nature's beauties has everywhere the sublime and beauti-ful; and, on looking down at the bottom of the hill towards the south-west, Loch Thom displays its infant pride, as if it had been one of those lakes which nature planted in its "bed of hill."

It is said that these hills abound with copper ore; and at a place called the Cove, a gentleman of science commenced, at an early period, the searching for this and other precious metals, which he declared the hill to abound with. About 1781, the labourers who were collecting the various springs reached this place, and discovered several implements hitherto unknown, and which were seen by the late Mr. Crawford, of Hillend. It is said that

Government interfered, and put a stop to the work. Tradition also says that there is a subterranean passage made, and by search will be found to exist, under the upper terrace where Watt's monument is to be fixed, communicating to that shaft or mine. A company, at a later period, began the search for copper ore; but this was abandoned, from the scanty supplies which they got.

In 1767 the first search for coal took place, and about five years ago various bores were made to a considerable depth; but the chance of success was so very unfavourable that it was abandoned. In regard to minerals, the Rev. Mr. A. Reid, in his "Statistical Account," published in 1793, says:—

"With respect to fossils, the parish of Greenock, as far as has been hitherto discovered, affords none that are any way remarkable Along the coast, freestone, mostly of a red colour, and sometimes beautifully variegated with regular spots of a light grey colour, occasionally inter-mixed with a great variety of what's called sea pebble, of different shapes and hues, is most common. The strata of this stone on the shore, and a great way above it, as if the vaults of caverns below them had some time failed, are very irregular, scarcely ever horizontal, but dipping or inclining at different angles in every direction, and chiefly towards the south. Limestone, though much needed for building and improvement of coarse stiff grounds, has only been of late discovered, and but in small quantities; nor is it of the best quality, being mixed with a considerable quantity of sand. Farther search, it is to be hoped, will be rewarded with better success. In the steep banks of some of the numer-ous rivulets from the hills, and in a thick bed of schistus, there appears a thin seam of it, divided into pieces about the size of a man's head, and of excellent quality. These, as they fall (for the expense of ground and labour would far exceed their value), are carefully collected, and used with good effect by the attentive farmer.

"Whether it would be advisable to make trial for coal in any part of the parish, those skilled in that business will be best able to determine. From the vast quantity used in Greenock and Port Glasgow, and annually exported by the merchants of both places, a mass of that necessary commodity would, it is evident, be a source of great wealth to the proprietor, and a very great benefit to the inhabitants of these towns and the places adjacent. In digging pretty deep wells, etc., there have occurred strata of earth, clay mixed with shells, sea sand, gravel, freestone, whin, etc., but no appearance hitherto of that valuable fossil. The hills, for the most part, seem to be a mass of whin, very compact and solid in some parts; in others, especially toward their summits, chinky and friable. In not a few places the rocks seem once to have been in a state of fusion, and loose stones scattered here and there exhibit so much the appearance of the cinders of a smithy furnace, that there can be little doubt of their having undergone, some time or other, the action of fire. What minerals the Greenock hills may contain is not known. The deep chasms made in them by sundry rivulets, which, after heavy rains, descend in torrents, have been carefully examined. In the drought of summer, the loose stones, pebbles, and sand, in the channel of these streams, have been examined by the writer of this sketch; but excepting ironstone of a poor quality, which is frequently found, and a little copper rarely in freestone, no metallic substance has been hitherto discovered."

Of the soil he also observes:—

"The soil, close upon the shore, is, in general, very light, sandy, and full of gravel, requiring frequent showers to produce tolerable pasture. After rest, however, and the aid of a little manure in favourable seasons, sea ware, for instance, of which from time to time, by strong westerly and northerly gales, there is no small quantity thrown on the shore, it produces very good crops of oats and barley; and, which annually becomes a great object of culture, large quantities of potatoes of the best quality. In the ascent, to a considerable distance from the flat ground on the shore, there occur soils of various kinds, earth, clay, till, etc. Farther up, and towards the summits of the hills seen from the shore, the soil for the most part is thin, in some places mossy; the bare rocks here and there appearing. On the other side of these hills, except a few cultivated spots in the ascent to and on the banks of Grife, heath, commonly tall, and a coarse benty grass prevail."

Since the period this was written, labour has certainly done much for the soil. We have as beautiful and fertile spots as can be found anywhere; while the specimens of flowers, fruits, etc., as reared in the open air, and exhibited at the horticultural societies, are not only nearly as early as other places, but of equal quality and beauty.—Mr. Reid goes on to state, that,

"The uncultivated part of the parish affords pasture for black cattle and sheep, and abounds with the different sorts of game common in this part of the country. In severe and continued frosts, vast flocks of wild ducks repair to the frith for their subsistance, and in snow, sometimes large flights of rooks frequent the shores. The food of the former is long grass, for which they dive to a considerable depth; of the latter, *wilks* or periwinkles, which having raised about fifty feet, they let fall among stones, stooping instantly after their prey. If the shell is not broke, they lift it again and again. Their toil is amazing, and their gain very small where there is as much wind as carries the wilk out of its perpendicular direction. Frauds in this business, as well as in that of building their nests, are attempted among them, which, when discovered, meet with instant and condign punishment.

"To this, and other hints of natural curiosities in the parish, given above, several others might be added. From the scooping of the rooks, for instance, a good way above high water mark, the fine polish of the gravel, and shells of the same kind with those which are at this time found on the shore, it is evident that the sea has greatly receded. The contexture of sea-pebbles, as they are called, which are scattered on some parts of the shore, and some pretty large blocks of greyish whin, scarcely yielding to any force but that of gunpowder, and in texture resembling Shakespeare's 'unwedgeable and gnarled oak,' it will not be easy to account for, on the principles of any of those theories of the earth, which in succession have been, with too much confidence, ushered into the world. Though some of the springs, with which the Greenock hills abound, are, in some degree, impregnated with iron, in general they emit the purest water, which is collected into sundry reservoirs, and thence conducted, in leaden pipes, to the different parts of the town. In widening the crevices of the rocks, from which the water issues, one is surprised to observe sometimes ten or a dozen frogs of different sizes, and of a dark colour, forced into day by the increased stream. Whether they are natives of the place from whence they came, entered in their tadpole state, or soon after, it is certain, that if the opening had not been enlarged, they could not have gone out; and it is remarkable, a circumstance on which one might moralise, that all of them make the utmost effort to return to their cold dark dungeon."

*   *   *   *   *

Chapter 14.
COMMUNICATION & STEAM-BOATS.

THE communication which Greenock had with other places, till about 1812, was with sailing packets and coaches.

Six coaches used to run regularly between Greenock and Glasgow, independent of the tedious passage by covered boats, called "fly-boats"; but which used often to occupy a day and a half in what is now done by steam in little more than two hours, since the introduction of steam-boats, the first of which, the Comet, appeared on the Clyde in 1812. This was the first built in the kingdom, and plied regularly between Glasgow and Greenock. The person who built this boat was Henry Bell, who, we are happy to state, has at length been rewarded according to his merits, by a pension from Government, as well as private donations.

The steamboats which now ply upon the Clyde are numerous; and some of them built by our ship-carpenters here are truly beautiful models. They, as well as our ships, are admired wherever they go, for the fine taste which has planned and executed them.

The largest steam-vessel built, and certainly the most beautiful, was the United Kingdom; we have already said she was launched from Messrs. Robert Steele & Co.'s building-yard. The next in size was the Chieftain, built by R. & A. Carsewell. It was from this port that the first steam-vessels which navigated the open sea between Dublin and Holyhead, were fitted out, and subsequently those which run betwixt the Clyde and Mersey. Steam-vessels leave our harbours regularly for Dublin, Liverpool, Belfast, and Derry, independent of those which call at the intermediate ports. In 1827 the number which plied was estimated at about sixty, and in 1829 they certainly have not decreased.

*   *   *   *   *

Chapter 15.
THE PROFESSIONAL CLASS.

IN bringing this work nearly to a close, we cannot but allude to the only institution in Greenock incorporated by Royal Charter, and which has been the means of doing much good to the trade of the Clyde, from the attention which has always been paid to communications, &c., emanating from this body:

The Chamber of Commerce was instituted in 1813 by a Royal Charter. The first directors were:—

Alexander Dunlop	John Denniston
James Leitch	James Watt
Archibald Baine	James Ritchie
John M'Naught	James Kippen
Robert Ewing	Greshom Stewart
Hugh Hamilton	John Dunlop
John Buchanan, jun.	

The object of this institution is to consider of, and suggest, such plans and systems as may contribute to the protection and improvement of those branches of commerce and manufactures with which they may be connected, or think conducive to the interest of the country.

The labours of this society, which have been considerable, embrace a great variety of business connected with public affairs, or with the peculiar concerns of the trade of the Clyde.

An important class in every community are the medical practitioners; and here they stand very high as to professional skill and acquirement. The following are the names of those who practised here, from the earliest period to the time of Dr. Ewing:

Dr. Cunningham, who survived the two following (Mr. W. Wilson and Mr. Love) died in 1769. Mr. Love published a paper, entitled "Observations on the Effects of Lignum Guacum in Cancer," in the 5th volume of the Medical Essays, printed in 1735. Mr. Wilson was father to Mr. Nathan Wilson, who succeeded him in practice, and was himself succeeded by his son William. Mr. Gavin Fullarton died in 1795; and Mr. David Colquhoun in 1807, Dr. John Colquhoun succeeded his fathers and died in 1817. Mr. P. Bruce and Dr. Ewing, both died young.

The following are those at present practising here:—

Andrew Hill, M.D.	James Mackay, M.D.
John Speirs, M.D.	John Speirs, Surgeon
John Simpson, Surgeon	David Patrick, Surgeon
J. B. Kirk, M.D.	John King, M.D.
Ninian Hill, M.D.	Frederick Gordon, Surgeon
Archibald Robertson, M.D.	John Hull, Surgeon
William Turner, Surgeon	Charles Auld, Surgeon

The writers in Greenock were, for a number of years, united into a society, by the name of "The Society of Writers in Greenock;" and upon a branch of the Sheriff Court being established in Greenock, they obtained a Charter, or Seal of Cause, from the late Sir Michael Shaw Stewart, incorporating them, under the name and style of "The Faculty of Procurators in Greenock." The charter is dated 20th January, 1816, and under it a variety of bye-laws were made by the faculty, as to the admission of procurators, yearly contributions for the support of widows, etc.; which were acted upon until within the last two or three years, when, some of the members becoming dissatisfied with the regulations of the faculty, the widows' fund, which had been accumulated to about

£600, was latterly divided; so that the society may now be considered as virtually dissolved. The faculty had a good library, which is still supported by a great majority of the procurators.

The following is a list of writers at present amongst us:

Robert Steuart.	Sam. Gemmell.	W. Johnston.
Wm. Kerr.	James Turner.	Wm. Currie.
Allan Swan.	Arch. Yuill.	Jos. Linton.
John Lamont.	John Black.	Robert Blair.
Geo. Williamson.	Dav. Glassford.	James Spiers, jr.
John Dunlop.	Wm. Liddell.	James Dunlop.
Arch. M'Kinnon,	James Turner, jr.	William Service.
John Paton.	Andrew Ingles.	
David Crawford.	Crawfurd Muir.	

*   *   *   *   *

Chapter 16.
CHRONOLOGY OF GREENOCK: 1739-1802.

THE following facts connected with Greenock have been chrono-
logically arranged from 1739 to 1802; and though not embodied
in the history itself, may be of sufficient consequence to interest
the reader. It was intended to bring them down to the present
time, but, as this would cause repetition, it has not been done.

1739.—Dreadful hurricane, when 14 vessels were driven on
shore, and one vessel, the Happy Union, came with such
violence above M'Gilp's Point (Open Shore), as to knock
down the gable of a Mrs. Weir's house, while the family
were at breakfast. This occurred on 13th January. Five boats
smuggling brandy were cast on shore, and all hands
perished.

1746.—General Campbell orders twelve pieces of cannon, to put
Inveraray in a state of defence.
18th July.—Elizabeth Orr arrived from Morlaix. Saw an
Irish wherry land 30 rebel officers; who, on being landed,
were greeted by the populace with "Vive Le Roi," imagining
Prince Charles to be of the party. They immediately sung,
"And a-begging we must go."
August.—Every house in Greenock searched by constables,
in consequence of information being sent to Edinburgh that
Prince Charles was here.

1750.—On the 30th of January they had the highest tide at Greenock that had been known these fifty years.

1751.—29th January. A duel fought behind Mr. Macfie's sugarhouse, between Lieutenant Legge and Mr. Russel, when the
latter was killed on the spot.

His Majesty gave the Royal Assent to the following Bill on
the 22nd May: "An Act for levying a duty of two pennies
Scots, or a sixth-part of a penny sterling, on every Scots pint
of Ale and Beer which shall be brewed for sale, brought into,
tapped, or sold within the town of Greenock, and Baronies of
Easter and Wester Greenock and Finnart, and liberties
thereof, in the County of Renfrew; for repairing the harbour
of the said town; and for other purposes therein mentioned."

1752.—October.—There was, about the middle of the month, the
largest take of herrings ever known off Port-Glasgow and
Greenock. Above 200 boats were employed in that fishery.
The fishes came up the frith in such shoals that, in one
morning, Captain Noble, of Farm, caught in his yare to the
value of twenty guineas and upwards.

East and Mid Quay first causewayed.

1756.—Weights for weighing tobacco got from Bristol, and a tax
laid upon each hogshead to defray expenses.

1757.—Damage was done in several places, on the evening of
March 23rd, by a storm, accompanied by thunder and lightning. At Greenock several vessels were drove from their
anchors and stranded.

1758.—Died at Greenock, 1st July, Captain C. Craig, of the
Ingram merchant-man. As the ship Betty was firing her guns
on her arrival from Jamaica, Captain Craig, then accidentally
walking on the quay, was unfortunately shot through the

belly by the wadding of one of them, and died in an hour after.

1760.—Edinburgh, February 23.—This morning an express from Captain Hay, regulating captain at Greenock, advises that the French squadron, under M. Thurot, left Islay on Tuesday, and on Wednesday entered the frith of Clyde, where they cruised for some time, and at last, upon a signal given, bore all away for the Irish coast, adding, that Lieutenant Paterson, whom he had despatched in a wherry to observe the enemy's motions had sent him notice, that on Thursday morning he came up with their squadron on the Irish coast, and saw them land at Carrickfergus a number of men, to the best of his observation not above 1500 nor under 1000.

The Ingram, Campbell, from Lisbon for Greenock, with wine and salt, taken February 20th, near Ailsa, by M. Thurot. The captain and crew were put ashore at Carrickfergus, and the ship sent for Bergen in Norway.

On May 20, the corpse of the late Duke of Argyle arrived at Greenock from London, and on Thursday morning, May 21, was put on board the barge of the family, which was decorated with standards and escutcheons, and the armorial bearings of the family. The barge was attended by thirteen other barges, all properly decorated, in which were the relations and friends of the family, who attended the corpse to Kilmun, the burial-place of the family, where it was deposited. During the whole time of the procession this day, minute guns were fired from Dumbarton Castle, and from the ships at Greenock and Port-Glasgow, and on the river. The procession by water was peculiarly grand and solemn.

1765.—Great distress, in consequence of the high price of meal, when the Magistrates and Sessions purchase for the poor.

Merchants agree to pay one half-penny on the hogshead of tobacco, to keep sheds in repair.

Edinburgh, March 20.—Yesterday, Matthew Jack, cooper, and Humphrey Ewing, porter, both in Greenock, were tried before the High Court of Justiciary, for abstracting the King's weights, and substituting light weights in the scale, at weighing tobaccos for exportation, thereby to defraud the revenue in the debentures to be granted on exportation. An unanimous verdict was returned, finding them guilty.

1766.—September 4.—The accounts we had formerly from Captain Aitken of Irvine, and Captain M'Cunn of this place, of a sunk rock near the entry of the north channel, are now confirmed by Captain Dunlop, of the Bogle, who arrived this day from Virginia, and gives the following accountably on the 29th ult., about four in the afternoon, he fell in with a small rock, bearing N. about a quarter of a mile, and, by the best computation they could make, lay about 60 leagues W. of Fillinghead, on the west coast of Ireland. Its top was ragged, and about the length of the ship's keel, and appeared about seven or eight feet above water; and, by an observation they had that day at noon, was exactly in the latitude of 55 degrees. They had a brisk gale at N.N.W., running six or seven knots, when they lost sight of it, which was in twenty minutes. It bore N.W. by W., distant about two-and-a-half miles.

1767.—May 25.—A few days ago, some people in this place, in searching for coal near Gourock, discovered a promising vein of copper ore, a little to the southward of Sir John Stuart of Castlemilk's house, several pieces of which they have brought hither, and, by a chemical operation, it proves to be very good. As it is found only two or three feet below ground, it is imagined that what they have seen is no more than branches from an extensive mine, lying seemingly in a direct line from Kempoch Point, near Gourock, to Longcraig, upwards of a mile south-east.

1773.—On Wednesday morning, January 20, a dreadful hurricane, accompanied with a little rain, did a great deal of damage in several places in Scotland; being the greatest that has been felt since the high wind in January, 1739. At Greenock the storm was very severe, where several ships were driven ashore and bilged, and some lives lost.

1775.—Town officer imprisoned and dismissed for allowing a prisoner to escape.

Bailie Gemmell writes Lord Cathcart to get the Magistrates made Justices of the Peace.

Magistrates and Council write Lord Cathcart to know the truth of a Collector and Comptroller being appointed here, and if it will be prejudicial to the interests of the port.

March 25.—Notwithstanding the disturbances in America, the spirit of emigration still unhappily prevails. This week a considerable number of labourers and useful mechanics from Monteith, Kippen, etc., some of them members of the Perth and Stirling Company, are gone down to Greenock, in order to embark for North America.

About the end of May, four vessels, containing about 700 emigrants, sailed for America from Port-Glasgow and Greenock, most of them from the North Highlands.

June 3.—Yesterday, before the sailing of the Monimia for New York, the officers of the customs divested the emigrants of all their firearms, swords, and daggers, before they went on board; by which prudent conduct the owners and freighters of the vessel were saved from the penalties

inflicted by the Act 29 Geo. II., for exporting arms, gunpowder, etc.

1776.—Additions made to West Burying Ground.

A ship sailed lately from Greenock for America, with shoes,
stockings, plaids, belts, etc., for a regiment of emigrants now
raising by government in America, to be called the "Royal
Highland Emigrants," Coats, arms, and ammunition are sent
from London.

About the middle of January, a government agent contracted
with some merchants of Glasgow and Greenock for upwards
of 7000 tons of shipping, to carry troops to America, and for
bedding, water casks, butcher meat, etc.

1777.—The Katie, Captain Clarke, and the Alison, Captain
Jamieson, two of the three armed vessels fitted out at Greenock, put to sea on the 19th of July, and returned on the 26th,
having seen none of the privateers during their cruise. The
third vessel was left behind, owing, it is said, to a trouble-
some fellow to whom she belonged, who was going to run
away with her, after the committee had manned and fitted
her completely.

1778.—Many towns in Scotland, on account of the revolt of the
American Colonies, assisted in promoting the recruiting
service, by offering bounties to persons residing within their
limits; some limited as to time and as to certain officers with
whom to enlist. Amongst these was the town of Greenock,
which offered two guineas a man for the Athol Highlanders,
in the company of Lord Cathcart, or that of his brother, Mr.
Charles.

Fifty-six French prisoners, the crews of prizes which had
been carried into Greenock by Scottish privateers, arrived at

Glasgow on the 18th, and at Edinburgh on the 23rd of November, under a guard of the Western Fencibles. They were lodged in apartments fitted up for them in Edinburgh Castle.

On information that our enemies intended to distress the west coast, train a of artillery—five nine-pounders and two six pounders—was sent from Edinburgh Castle for Green-ock, Sept. 5th; and 200 small arms, with the like number of cartouche boxes, etc., to arm the inhabitants of that town who voluntarily offered their services. At the same time, several bodies of troops marched to the same place.

Before the middle of October, nine privateers fitted out on the Clyde had sailed, and five more were almost ready to sail, carrying in whole upwards of 200 guns and 800 men.

1779.—Magistrates and Town Council most strenuously oppose the Catholic Claims. Afterwards Lord George Gordon visited Greenock, and received a gold box for his exertions in that cause. On the night of his acquittal the town was illuminated.

1781.—Wells first opened on a fair-day. Lamps first lighted.

1784.—Postage of a single letter from Edinburgh to Greenock, threepence.

On Friday, April 23, were committed to the tolbooth of Edinburgh, by warrant of the Judge of the High Court of Admiralty, James Herdman, John M'Iver, and Archibald M'Callum, merchants in Greenock. They are accused at the instance of Robert Hunter, Esq., and others, underwriters in London, with wilfully and feloniously sinking or destroying certain ships at sea, upon which Mr. Hunter and others had underwritten considerable sums; and for which offences

these gentlemen mean to bring them to trial capitally before
the Judge Admiral.—They were found guilty, and pilloried
at Glasgow.

The Gazette of 17th July contains notice, that information
has been transmitted by the Court of France to the Secretary
of State, that several of His Britannic Majesty's subjects are
detained in France as hostages for payment of ransoms.
Notice is given, that in case such ransom bills are not forthwith discharged, prosecutions will be commenced in the
Court of Admiralty against all masters, owners and others,
unjustly refusing or neglecting to pay the sums of money
stipulated for relief of those unfortunate persons, who have
suffered so long an imprisonment. The following are the
ships belonging to Greenock contained in the list:—

Ships and Captains.	Place.	Hostages.	Ransom Sums.
Fortitude.. Johnston	Greenock	C. Kennedy	1500 Guineas
John......... Crawford	do.	D. White	50 do.
Bell Bange	do.	A. Stewart	50 do.

1787.—August 21.—The take of herrings from the Garvel Perch
to Finlayston Point, and even to Dumbarton Castle, is
amazing, since the 15th instant. They are sold from eight-
pence to one shilling per hundred, for salting and for the red
herring house at Gourock; and the dealers in herrings come
down here, and salt up vast quantities in orange and lemon
boxes, which they carry through the country on carts for
sale.

1791.—On the 21st March the ship Brunswick was launched
from Messrs. Scott & Co.'s building yard. She measures
about 600 tons carpenter's tonnage, may carry about 1000
tons real burden, and is supposed to be the largest vessel

built in Scotland since the Union. She is built for the New Brunswick and Nova Scotia trade.

1795.—The following singular excursion was performed by Captain M'Alpine.—He set out from Greenock in a small boat with a party, and sailed up Lochlong; and having got their boat carried over in a cart, about two miles from the head of Lochlong, to Lochlomond, sailed down the Loch and Water of Leven up to the Broomielaw of Glasgow, and returned safe to Greenock.

1796.—The storm on Saturday, the 23rd January, was uncommonly severe on the west coast, accompanied with very high tides at Greenock. It was accompanied with a great deal of thunder and lightning. None of the shipping, however, we are happy to say, suffered any damage. For two days previous the tides were remarkably high, but on the 25th there was the highest ever remembered. All the quays and breasts were covered completely, and the dry dock was filled by the overflow of the waters.

The Dutch frigate, Jason, mounting 36 guns, with upwards of 200 men on board, was on the 8th inst. brought into Greenock by her crew, who had put their officers under confinement. This frigate is part of a Dutch squadron which sailed from the Texel in February last; but, having met with damages, was obliged to put into Drontheim to refit. A great party of the Sutherland Fencibles have marched from Glasgow to Greenock to take possession of the frigate.

1799.—A dreadful fire broke out at Greenock in a sailcloth maker's, on the 16th March, which did great damage. Besides the houses, upwards of 600 bolls of wheat, 100 puncheons of rum, 400 bags of sugar, and many other articles, were consumed.

April 4.—The two O'Connors, Dr. M'Niven, and the other State prisoners who arrived from Ireland a few days ago, were escorted from Greenock, on their route to Fort-George, by Major Hay and a detachment of the North York Militia. They are twenty in all,—sixteen from Dublin and four from Belfast. They are completely cropped, and all wear moustaches in the French style.

1801.—Such is the flourishing state of the commerce of the Clyde, that there were employed in the trade of Greenock alone, in the year ending 5th January last, 175,551 tons of shipping; and the revenue of customs for the same period was L.180,341 1s. 81d. Sterling.

The population of Greenock in 1801 was 17,458.

1802.—The population of Greenock increases so rapidly, that notwithstanding the many new buildings, many poor families could not procure houses at this term, and have been obliged to take up their abode in barns and out-houses.

Mr. Noel, Member of the French National Institute, arrived at Greenock last week. He is, we understand, preparing for the press a "Natural History of the Herring;" and the object of his visit to Greenock is to add to his stock of knowledge on the subject, by conversing with Mr. Hugh Crawfurd, whose known attention to the business of the fisheries pointed him out as well qualified to furnish the desired information.

*   *   *   *   *

Chapter 17.
TOURS OF THE AREA & CONCLUSION.

THE documents connected with this history having been nearly exhausted, it now only remains to give a short sketch of the various pleasure tours which can be accomplished in a short period from our harbour. And there is scarcely any situation round about more centrical for embarking on a tour of pleasure for two days or as many weeks; while the convenience of our inns, and their excellent management, ensure every comfort.

The first of these is the delightful excursion to Helensburgh, the Gareloch, and Roseneath. The usual way is by steam to this fashionable watering village; and from this you can walk up the banks of the Loch to the Row Ferry, and from thence cross to Roseneath. The scenery from this extensive peninsula is of the most sublime description, combining, as it does, many beautiful scenes of high cultivation; all of which are bounded with a ridge of finely marked hills. Before leaving this spot, it is worth while visiting the mansion of the Duke of Argyle. Though in an unfinished state, it has still a princely appearance. The next tour to Lochgoilhead and Arrochar can be accomplished by Dumbarton; and by embracing this route, the Vale of Leven, with its winding stream, and the exquisite scenery of Lochlomond, with its many islands and lofty Ben, can all be seen. If the traveller wishes to extend his journey beyond the day, he can turn to the right from Inversnaid Mill, and from thence visit the old fort of Inversnaid, as also Locharkil, Loch Catharine, and Trossachs, with their rich and unrivalled scenery; and from thence continue the route either by Aberfoyle, or by Lochs Achray and Venacher, through Callender on to Stirling, which can be accomplished in about two days. The route which turns from the left at Lochlomond, is a narrow stripe of land, which divides its waters from those of Lochlong. Having reached Arrochar, here the scenery is of the wildest description; and Benarthur lifts its abrupt top towards the west. The sail down Lochlong is truly interesting; but probably the best winding-up of the tour is to proceed through Glencroe on to Inverary. This leads through that bleak and barren vale, with its ragged crags, till you reach Lochrestal, in the vicinity of which is a stone inscribed with "Rest and be thankful." Proceeding onwards, the road varies, and assumes an interesting appearance, till you reach Arkinglas, and from this cross Lochfyne to Invera- ray at St. Catherines. The pleasure grounds around the Duke's castle are extensive and well planned. The hill of Dunicoich, which stands behind the castle, has a fine appearance. The castle was begun in 1745, and has been much improved; and is well worthy of being visited by the stranger. On leaving Inveraray, the route can be pursued down Lochfyne, and along the picturesque scenery of the Kyles of Bute; or from Strachur on the opposite side, along Locheck, till you reach Holy Loch.

The work is now brought to a close; and though it embraces but a short period, has many facts which may be interesting to those who are natives, residing here or in a foreign land. Many of these particulars have been gleaned from old inhabitants, who still remember the beginning of almost all our streets, and when not a single spire or stalk reared its head. The change has been wonderful; and to those who, after thirty years' absence, have again visited their early scenes and schoolboy haunts, the effect of this has been almost overpowering. That love of country which is the distinguishing characteristic of almost every Scotsman, in whatever clime, or under whatever circumstances their lot may be cast, is considered very powerful in those who have left our shores, and, through various circumstances, been compelled to seek wealth and honours in other lands. If these few pages recall to them anything of the past, or stir up a kind remembrance, one object of this book has been accomplished. And to those who remain, none amongst them can wish more fervently for a union of feeling, in looking to the interests of the community, and to the growing importance of our native town, than the compiler of these pages, who now concludes this history in the beautiful lines of Sir Walter Scott:—

> "Breathes there a man, with soul so dead,
> Who never to himself hath said
> This is my own, my native land!
> Whose heart hath ne'er within him burn'd,
> As home his footsteps he hath turn'd,
> From wandering on a foreign strand!
> If such there breathe, go, mark him well;
> For him no Minstrel raptures swell;
> High though his titles, proud his name,
> Boundless his wealth as wish can claim;
> Despite those titles, power, and pelf,
> The wretch, concentred all in self,
> Living, shall forfeit fair renown,
> And, doubly dying, shall go down
> To the vile dust, from whence he sprung,
> Unwept, unhonour'd, and unsung."

*　　　*　　　*　　　*　　　*

NOTE 1, page 2.

THE derivation of the name GREENOCK is from "Chalmers' Caledonia." Mr. Williamson has written an ingenious letter, proving that "Graenaig," meaning a sunny bay, is the proper derivation. In this he has also the authority of Mr. Reid, in the "Statistical Account;" and this is probably the most correct.

NOTE 2, page 26-7.

An account is given of the poor's rates for 1829. In Mr. Reid's Statistical work are the following remarks on this subject for 1793:—

"The funds for the maintenance of the poor, who are very numerous, are the weekly collections at the churches, the Marine Society, and the trades boxes. These being inadequate, and to put a stop to vagrant begging, with which the town was intolerably infested, the inhabitants of both parishes, In 1785, agreed to assess themselves in a sum that might supply the deficiency. The scheme, which has been conducted as the law directs, has been continued; and, but for the simplicity of people who still give encouragement to vagrants, would completely answer its important end. The sum raised by assessment from the beginning has not greatly increased. The assessment for 1791 was £360. Where there are many separate funds for the maintenance of the poor, it is not to be supposed that an equal distribution can be made. It Is therefore much to be wished, that as many of them as possibly could, were thrown into one, for the benefit of the indigent. The annual amount of charities in Greenock is not less, it is believed, than £1200 Sterling."

NOTE 3, page 57—the Slaughter-house.

The number of cattle killed at the Slaughterhouse last year was, 1165 cows, 1139 calves, 9385 sheep, 8816 lambs, 4 goats, and 106 swine.

In 1815 it stood thus—2391 cows, 15,105 sheep, 8500 lambs, and 285 swine.

NOTE 4, page 79—upwards of 9,000 pounds.

It is stated, that in 1819 the revenues from the Harbour exceeded £9000 per annum. This year the amount stands thus—

Harbour Duty,....................................	£5226	9	2
From Sheds, ...	2318	17	6
From Steamboats,..............................	1308	7	6
From New Dock, ...	889	0	5
From Anchorage and Ring Money,...	794	3	7
Harbour Police to Cr..........................	706	17	2
	£11,243	15	4

NOTE 5, page 114—Shipbuilding by Scott.

It is to be regretted that the list of Mr. Scott's tonnage of ship-building goes no farther back than 1802, though the business was begun in 1773. The vessels built since that period amount in tonnage to 16,800, of square and fore-and-aft-rigged vessels and steamers. There is at present a fine ship on stocks, to be called the "John Scott;" the full-length figure-head of which is an excellent likeness, and has been cut by our talented townsman, Mr. A. Robertson[1] of Liverpool.

NOTE 6, page 114—Shipbuilding by Carsewell.

Messrs. R. & A. Carsewell's tonnage of shipping in all amounts to 2992, including the "Hugh Crawford," a fine cutter of 60 tons, launched a few lays ago.

---

1. Archibald Robertson was the artist who carved the famous likeness of Habbie Simpson, the Piper of Kilbarchan. Interested readers should refer to MUCH ABOUT KILMACOLM, published by THE GRIAN PRESS, 2004.—GP

Alexander, John, R. N.
Aytoun, Roger.
Allan, William.
Angus, Robert.
Athol, Captain.
Aitken, Thomas.
Allan, John, New York.
Aitken, William.

Brown, Neil.
Bain, Archibald, Jun.
Balderston, David.
Baird, James.
Blair, George.
Brown, Rev. Thomas.
Brymner, A.
Blackwood, William, 2 copies
Buchanan, Robert, Edinburgh.
Buchanan, Colin.
Bissland, Thomas.
Black, John.
Ballantine, James.
Buchanan, John.
Boyd, John, Edinburgh.
Blair, James.
Blair, Duncan.
Brownlie, William.
Barefoot, Mr., London.
Bunten, Thomas, 6 copies.
Brown, J. L., 3 copies.
Bowie, Malcolm.
Buchanan, John, Cooper.
Brown, Rev. Mr.
Buchanan, Neil.
Brown, John, Halifax.
Bain, Archibald, Jun.

Cathcart, Earl.
Carswell, Robert.

Clark, John.
Carmichael, James.
Cameron, Hugh.
Carmichael, Thomas.
Caird, James.
Caird, John.
Currie, William.
Crawford, David.
Carswell, Alexander.
Clark, Andrew.
Cunningham, Wm., Port-Glasgow.
Cadell & Co., Edinburgh.
Campbell, John, Customs.
Chatfield, Captain, R. C.
Campbell, Alexander, Ballochyle.
Cambridge, Archibald.
Cunningham, William, Glasgow.
Campbell, Archibald.
Carss, John.
Carter, Rev. W. D.
Campbell, John.
Chisholm, William.

Darroch, General.
Darroch, Captain.
Dunlop, Hutchison.
Dunlop, John.
Dennistoun, John.
Dupuis, Gasper.
Dennistoun, John, Jun.
Dunlop, Alexander, Keppoch.
Dempster, George.
Dempster, John.
Dunlop, Captain, R. N.
Dunn, James.
Duncan, Alexander, Aberdeen.
Dobie, James, Beith.
Dunlop, James.

Ewing, Robert.

Farquhar, Robert, London.
Ferguson, George, 2 copies.
Ferguson, Dr., R.N.
Fleming, John.
Fisher, John.
Finlay, Alexander.
Fletcher, Angus, Dunoon.
Frazer, James.
Fisher, James.
Farquhar, John.
Fisher, William.

Gordon, Rev. John.
Griffin, Richard, Glasgow, 5 copies
Gairdner, James, Glasgow.
Gellie, Miss.
Geils, Major.
Galbraith, James.
Gray, John K.
Grahame, John.
Gardiner, John.

Hart, Thomas.
Hunter, James, Hafton.
Heron, John, 3 copies.
Heron, William, 3 copies.
Hunter, Peter.
Hutton, Hugh.
Hislop, John.
Harvie, James, Glasgow.
Harvie, David.
Harvie, William.
Hood, James.
Hamilton, George.
Hamilton, L. G., Teneriffe.
Hunter, Robert.
Hall, Mrs. Clayton, Brighton.

Henderson, John, Kinross.
Hamilton, Hugh.
Henderson George.
Haddow, John.

Inglis, Andrew, 3 copies.

Jeffray, Francis, Advocate.
Jackson, Peter.
Jones, Captain.
Johnstone, George.
Johnston, Adam.
Johnston, Adam, Jun.
Johnston, William.
Johnston, William, printer.
Johnston, William, writer.
Johnston, J. W., Derry.

Kirk, Dr.
King, Matthew, Port-Glasgow.
Kerr, William.
Keats, Captain, R. N.
Kay, Peter, Edinburgh.
Kayser, J. C.
Kelly, James.
Kerr, James.
Kippen, James.
Kilbie, R. S. G.
Kuhll, Nicholas.

Lindsay, Andrew.
Leitch, James.
Leitch, William.
Leitch, Robert.
Lade, William, Port-Glasgow.
Laing, Andrew.
Lang, Thomas.
Lindsay, W. A.
Lumsden, James,Glasgow, 5 copies.

Lumsden, John,Glasgow, 5 copies.
Lyle, Robert.
Leckie, James M.,Dublin, 6 copies.
Lyon, Malcom. Lawson, Captain.
Lindsay, Robert.
Lamont, Colin, Jun., 2 copies.
Liddell, William, Jun.
Liddell, Andrew.
Logan, George.
Leitch, John, Rothsay.
Leitch, Captain John.

Mennons, John.
Murray, Robert.
Miller, John, Savannah.
Munro, George, Glasgow.
Miller, Andrew L., Savannah.
Muir, Crawford.
Muir, James.
Marshall, Claud.
Mitchell, P. M., Dumbarton.
Marquis, John, jun.
Moore, V. H.
Morrison, John.
Morrison, James.
Maxton, Captain.
Muston, T. P., Genoa.
Marshall, V. B., R.N.
Morren, Rev. N.
Menzies, Rev. V.
Munn, James, Islay.
Munro, John.
Moodie, Miss.
Muir, Andrew.
M'Callum, Peter.
M'Cunn, John.
M'Cunn, Thomas, Jun.
M'Lellan, John.
M'Lellan, John, Jun.

M'Pherson, Captain.
M'Donald, James, Glasgow.
M'Lellan, R.
M'Phail, H.
M'Donald, James.
M'Cunn, David, Jamaica.
M'Cunn, James, Jamaica.
M'Farlane, Robert.
M'Nab, John.
M'Briar, James.
M'Iver, Archibald, 2 copies.
M'Dowall, William.
M'Kellar, Dugald.
M'Cunn, John.
M'Fie, John, Leith.
M'Fie, William, of Langhouse.
M'Leish, Adam.
M'Dermott, Rev. A., Galway.
M'Farlan, John.
M'Lachlan. C., Van Dieman'sLand.
M'Lellan, Ronald, Glasgow.
M'Viccar, Archibald, 2 copies.i
Mackay, Rev. Mackintosh,L.L.D.
M'Goun, John.
M'Ewen, Dugald.
M'Kinnon, Archibald.
M'Cunn, Archibald.
M'Cunn, Robert, Glasgow.
M'Farlane, Daniel.
M'Farlane, John,Customs, 2 copies.
M'Kechnie, Mrs.
M'Phedran, Archibald, 2 copies.
M'Cunn, John, Customs.
M'Lellan, Murdoch, Milton.
M'Donald, John, Pable.
M'Grigor, James.
M'Kenzie, John.
M'Cunn, Thomas.
M'Nab, Robert.

M'Kellar, Archibald.
M'Naughtan, John.
M'Laurin, Alexander.
M'Arthur, Neil.
M'Cormick, Alexander.

Newman, A. K., London.
Noble, George.
Newton, Captain, 2 copies.
Nicoll, Thomas.
Neill, John.

Oliver & Boyd, 2 copies.
Oughterson, James.

Paton, John, Writer.
Park, John 2 copies.
Paton, David.
Paton, John.
Paul, Daniel.

Robinson, J. O., London.
Robertson & Atkinson, Glasgow.
Rochefort, Capt., R. N.
Ritchie, R. P., Belfast.
Robertson, Archibald, M. D.
Robertson, Rev. A.
Robertson, George.
Robertson, John, Glasgow.
Robertson, J. H., 3 copies.
Robertson, James, Edin., 3 copies.
Robertson, John, Derry.
Ross, Capt.
Ross, Alexander.
Robertson, George, London.
Robertson, James, Liverpool.
Ryder, James, R. N.
Ralston, Robert.
Robertson, William.

Robson, John.
Robertson, Archibald, Liverpool.

Scott, Sir Walter, Bart.
Stewart, Sir M. S., Bart.
Stewart, Lady Shaw.
Stewart, Capt. H., R.N.
Stewart, J. S., Edinburgh.
Stewart, P.M., London.
Stewart, Sir James, Bart.
Scott, William, 2 copies.
Stirling & Kenny, Edin., 10 copies.
Steele, James.
Stuart, James.
Scott, Christopher.
Speirs, Dr.
Scott, Wm., Ship Chandler.
Stewart, Capt., R. N.
Swan, Joseph.
Sword, Archibald.
Sharp, Daniel.
Sinclair, John, London.
Shairpe, Capt., R. N.
Shaw, James, Edinburgh.
Stewart, Capt., R. C.
Stewart, James, Beltrees.
Stevenson, James, Sen.
Sinclair, Robert, 2 copies.
Steele, Rev. Robert.
Stewart, Andrew.
Steele, William.
Scott, Charles C.
Scott, John.
Scott, John, Jun.
Simons, William, 2 copies.
Scott, Wm., Bookseller, 6 copies.
Stewart, James, 2 copies.
Stewart, William.
Swell, William, R. N.

Snell, J. C., R. N.
Steele, Robert, Jun. 2 copies.
Sinclair, Alexander, Loudon.
Speirs, James.
Speirs, John, Surgeon.

Turner, William, Surgeon.
Tasker, James.
Thomson, John, Edinburgh.
Thomson, Alexander, 5 copies.
Turner, James.
Thomson, John.
Thom, Robert, 6 copies.
Thom, James.
Todd, George.

Urie, Matthew.

Wood, Sir Gabriel.
Walker, William.
Whyte, John.

Watt, James.
Wharton, John.

Wilson, Archibald.
Wark, Morrison.
Weir, Duncan, 2 copies.
Walker, John.
Wilson, Archibald, Glasgow.
Walshe, R. Weldon, M. R. I. A.
Watt, James, jun.
Waugh & Innes, Edin. 2 copies.
Watson, John.
Weir, Robert, 6 copies.
Walkinshaw, James.
Watson, James.
Watson, William, 6 copies.
Weir, John.
Weir, John.
Whittaker, Geo., London, 25 copies.
Walker, Hugh.

Yuill, Archibald.
Young, William, Edinburgh.
Young, Maitland.
Young, Archibald, Glasgow.

Printed in the United Kingdom
by Lightning Source UK Ltd.
103108UKS00001B/13-33